EKG

EMPOWERING   KINGDOM   GROWTH

THE HEARTBEAT
OF
GOD

D0289903

LifeWay Press®
Nashville, Tennessee

Published by LifeWay Press®
© 2004 • Kenneth S. Hemphill
Third Printing • April 2005

ISBN: 0-6331-9758-0

This book is a resource in the Personal Life category of the Christian Growth Study Plan.
Course CG-1062

Dewey Decimal Classification Number: 231
Subject Heading: GOD \ CHRISTIAN LIFE

Unless otherwise noted, all Scripture quotations are taken from the *Holman Christian Standard Bible*®
Copyright © 1999, 2000, 2002, 2004 by Holman Bible Publishers.
Used by permission.

We believe the Bible has God for its author; salvation for its end; and truth, without any mixture of error, for its matter and that all Scripture is totally true and trustworthy.
The 2000 statement of *The Baptist Faith and Message* is our doctrinal guideline.

To order additional copies of this resource: WRITE LifeWay Church Resources Customer Service;
One LifeWay Plaza; Nashville, TN 37234-0113; FAX order to (615) 251-5933;
PHONE (800) 458-2772; ORDER ONLINE at *www.lifeway.com;*
or VISIT the LifeWay Christian Store serving you.

Printed in the United States of America

Leadership and Adult Publishing
LifeWay Church Resources
One LifeWay Plaza
Nashville, Tennessee 37234-0175

Contents

Introduction

The kingdom of God is real. It is past, it is present, and it is future. The kingdom is the rule and reign of God, and you become a kingdom person when you make the decision to accept Jesus Christ as Lord and Savior of your life.

EKG: The Heartbeat of God, based on the Broadman & Holman book by Ken Hemphill, *Empowering Kingdom Growth: The Heartbeat of God,* is A 40 Day Experience to help you become aware of the kingdom God all around you and your role as a kingdom citizen. From this study you will:

- See where in Scripture the kingdom begins.
- Begin to read the Bible with a new kingdom perspective.
- See yourself as God's much-loved movable possession.
- Learn the meaning of kingdom praying.
- Gain new understanding of Jesus' Sermon on the Mount as you look at it through a kingdom lens.
- Discover that your life, your family, and your church can take on greater meaning and purpose when you determine to make kingdom living a priority.

EKG: THE HEARTBEAT OF GOD LEADER KIT

It is recommended that each small-group leader have an *EKG: The Heartbeat of God Leader Kit.* Each kit contains a copy of this study; *Empowering Kingdom Growth: The Heartbeat of God* (Broadman & Holman), by Ken Hemphill, on which this 40 Day Experience is based; a DVD featuring the author teaching on these topics; and a CD with an administrative guide and outlines (guide and outlines also available at www.*lifeway.com/a40dayexperience)* and manuscripts for sermons that relate to every week of the 40 Day Experience.

 This symbol indicates when to show the DVD segment in each small-group session.

SMALL-GROUP SESSIONS

This 40 Day Experience resource contains seven small-group sessions, each designed for group members to participate, whether or not they have attended previous sessions. One of the main benefits of this weekly small-group and daily devotional experience is allowing your small-group and your congregation to focus together on these important concepts.

The small-group sessions and devotions add up to a 40 day experience. In addition to the narrative, each small-group session and devotional has interactions marked with symbols (described on the following page) that identify the purpose for each activity.

EK COMMUNITY

Experiencing Kingdom Community uses questions to help group members interact with and learn about one another.

EK TRUTH

Experiencing Kingdom Truth provide help to guide group members examine Bible passages.

EK CHALLENGE

Experiencing Kingdom Challenge encourages group members to apply biblical truths to their lives.

EK LOVE

Experiencing Kingdom Love suggests ways for group members to show love and concern for one another and for people outside their small group.

EK PRAYER

Experiencing Kingdom Prayer directs participants to communicate with God about a need revealed in the session.

**EK
KNOWLEDGE**

Experiencing Kingdom Knowledge assists group members in understanding the meaning of Scripture.

SERMON NOTES

If your pastor and church worship services are also focusing on the *EKG* 40 Day Experience, you should take sermon notes to enhance your learning and spiritual growth. Sermon Notes pages are provided for this purpose.

DEVOTIONALS

Six of the small-group sessions are followed by daily devotionals that reinforce the truths in each sessions. Each devotional ends with a challenge.

The Heartbeat of God

The kingdom is the rule and reign of God.

What is the kingdom of God? What does it mean to be a kingdom person? These two questions have changed the way I live. They have reached into every single area of my life, leaving nothing untouched, transforming even the most ordinary transactions of my day into opportunities charged with meaning and potential. In the kingdom of God, I have found something far superior to personal fulfillment. I have found the heart of God. I have found my reason for being here on earth.

1. Based on a country you have visited, a movie you have seen, or a book you have read, what are some characteristics of a kingdom?

EK COMMUNITY

2. If you lived in a country ruled by a king, what privileges and responsibilities might you have?

◆ Use the corresponding *EKG* DVD segment for this session now.

> **The Kingdom of God**
> God is the Creator and Ruler of everything. God's desire is for everyone to know He is their King and to love and obey Him as part of His eternal kingdom.
> We are going to cover this grand sweep of God's kingdom in this book. I want you to see that including us in His kingdom always has been God's purpose from day one.
> I want you to see the size and weight and enormity of God's rule and reign. I want you to get a taste of the freedom and excitement that grow out of living in God's grace and with God's perspective.

Read Matthew 6:33.
- What is "the kingdom of God"?

- What does putting the kingdom first mean to you?

> " 'But seek first the kingdom of God and His righteousness, and all these things will be provided for you' " (Matt. 6:33).

- How does "His righteousness" clarify what you should seek?

- As a kingdom citizen, if you seek God's kingdom, what "things" will be provided?

1. Describe a citizen of God's kingdom, who "seeks first the kingdom of God and His righteousness."

2. In your description is a kingdom citizen known by:

   - ❑ what he is (thinks, feels, believes);
   - ❑ what he is not (does not think, feel, believe);
   - ❑ what he does not do;
   - ❑ what he does?

3. Add to your description additional characteristics of a kingdom citizen.

4. Do you know someone you would label a "kingdom person"?

5. What actions most define you as a kingdom citizen?

- What actions can you and/or your small group take in the next day or two to show God's love to another?

THE KINGDOM QUEST

EK KNOWLEDGE

The kingdom refers to the rule and reign of God—a rule that has always existed, a reign that will exist forever. Jesus, spoke often of His kingdom in the future, when " 'many will come from east and west, and recline at the table with Abraham, Isaac, and Jacob in the kingdom of heaven' " (Matt. 8:11). Yet He could also say, with equal accuracy, that "if I drive out demons by the finger of God, then the kingdom of God has come to you" (Luke 11:20). This absolute control of God over all things will one day be visibly seen for the reality it is.

What are things you live with every day that are real but not visible?

1.   2.

3.   4.

God rules us. We are His. He orchestrates events and directs human history, while somehow—somehow—leaving intact our ability to make decisions and choose our own path. We can walk into each day fully aware by faith that every person we see, every article we read, and every question we are asked are all coming our way by the intention of the King.

God's kingdom is at work as we represent God (embody God's name), show His love to the world (embrace His mission), and live in His will (obey His Word). Name one way you can:

• Embrace His mission;

• Embody His name;

• Obey His Word.

The United States is the world's third largest nation in population with 290 million people. Only China and India have more people. Of the 290 million people in the United States, an estimated 213 million are lost. If only the lost population were considered, the United States would be the fourth largest country behind China, India, and Indonesia. (Source: NAMB)

Where do you see God at work in the world today?

Think of the kingdom as occurring in four linked time periods:

1. The Old Testament—Israel, the people of God, functioned as subjects of the King. He used them to display His love, mercy, and glory for the purpose of reaching the nations.

2. Jesus' life—The Christ, the Messiah, our Redeemer—became a living, breathing reality through Jesus' earthly ministry. He was God, our Ruler, in the flesh.

> **Church** spelled with a lower case "c" refers to the local body of believers you can worship with. **The church is** part of **the Church**, all the redeemed people of all the ages. List at least two ways you have seen God advance the kingdom by working through a local church. Discuss how God was visible in those actions. How did the kingdom grow?

3. The Church—The Church is not the same thing as the kingdom, but until Jesus comes again, God works through the Church to advance His kingdom in the world.

4. Christ's return—The final phase of the kingdom begins when Jesus Christ returns for His bride, the Church—His people. "He will reign forever and ever!" (Rev. 11:15), "and His kingdom will have no end" (Luke 1:33).

KINGDOM PERSON, KINGDOM MOMENT

The kingdom of God can make big changes in your life. To live in the kingdom will require you to alter your perspectives on a lot of the things. Kingdom living could mean

• relocation to another city or country;

• a job change, or some other major decision or event in your life;

• a new way of thinking about how you spend your free time.

Living as a kingdom person will open your eyes to the people in your routine. Being aware of the veiled importance of all the moments of your day reveals them as kingdom moments.

You will gain an accurate sense of being involved in something that will outlast and outlive you. Seeking the kingdom of God first and foremost will impact every area of your life.

Check ways to watch for the kingdom of God. Add one more that applies to your life.

- ❑ Listen to the news and read the paper with a new perspective.
- ❑ View the events of daily life with a kingdom focus.
- ❑ Look for a kingdom opportunity when standing in line at a checkout.
- ❑ View with different eyes the resources at your disposal.
- ❑ Begin to ask, "How can I use my home for kingdom purposes?"
- ❑ Work and play with new meaning.
- ❑ Do your job with even greater excellence and a kingdom goal.
- ❑ Raise your children intentionally preparing them for life in the kingdom.
- ❑ _____

> As you read this week's devotional thoughts and prepare for the next small-group session, for a more complete study, read the introduction and Section 1, "A King and His People," in *Empowering Kingdom Growth: The Heartbeat of God* (Nashville: Broadman & Holman, 2004).

Much is at stake! If you fail to grasp the meaning of the kingdom

- you will fail to understand what is most important to your Lord, what was on the heart of God from before the creation of the world;
- you will fail to see God's kingdom activity all around you;
- you will fail to enjoy the privilege of participating in supernatural work;
- you will fail to employ the available power of the Holy Spirit;
- you will miss the joy of knowing that you have pleased your Father;
- you will miss the exhilarating freedom that comes from radical obedience;
- you will miss the opportunity to experience God's abundant provision and will continue to be plagued by worry, fear, and anxiety.
- you will miss God's purpose for your life.

EK PRAYER When I think about what kingdom living could mean for you, your family, and your church, I am excited. When I think about the change it could bring about in your local community, I am hopeful. When I think about the impact such faithful obedience to God's Word could have on our world, I am overwhelmed. For the believer in Christ, living in the kingdom is the only reality.

- How can you pray for one another this week?

Scripture Text

Main Points

1.

2.

3.

Meaningful Illustrations

Personal Application

DAY 1

You Can

Before the Israelites could become useful as God's people, His unique possession, they had to experience God's redemption. There was no other way.

The same is true today. Do you know for certain that you have a personal relationship with God? Until you do, this kingdom message is going to cause you nothing but frustration. If God is dealing with you at this point, and you know in your heart that you have not surrendered your heart and life to Jesus Christ, you can do it right now.

1. Romans 3:23 states the problem clearly: "For all have sinned and fall short of the glory of God." We were created in God's image and designed to live in relationship with Him, but our sin has separated us from a holy God.

2. God has made a way for us to escape the penalty of sin. "For the wages of sin is death, but the gift of God is eternal life in Christ Jesus our Lord" (Rom. 6:23). This verse contains both the bad and the good news of the gospel. Sin leads to spiritual death, separating us from God. But eternal life in Christ is His gift to us. It is God's forgiveness that erases our sin. His forgiveness is a gift. It cannot be earned but must be received from God.

3. Jesus lived a sinless life and yet was crucified like a common criminal. Because of love, He paid the penalty for our sin. " 'For God loved the world in this way: He gave His One and Only Son, so that everyone who believes in Him will not perish but have eternal life' " (John 3:16). God the Father "made the One who did not know sin to be sin for us, so that we might become the righteousness of God in Him" (2 Cor. 5:21).

4. The Bible says, "If you confess with your mouth, 'Jesus is Lord,' and believe in your heart that God raised Him from the dead, you will be saved" (Rom. 10:9). You have probably heard these truths before. But hearing without believing is not enough. You must admit your sin and turn toward God, to serve Him as your rightful King.

EK PRAYER You may want to pray this prayer: "Father, I have sinned against You. I am sorry for my sin, and I turn from it today. I believe that Jesus died for my sin and was raised to give me life. I invite Him to come into my heart and save me. Amen."

Obedience

DAY 2

When the Israelites left Egypt and headed to the promised land, God offered them a covenant relationship. Moses explained it to the people this way: if they were going to enjoy the land of promise, obedience would have to pave the way. If they were going to partake in the blessings of kingdom living, faithfulness to God and His laws would have to come first.

Let's listen in on a few of Moses' instructions:

- "Therefore, love the Lord your God and always keep His mandate and His statutes, ordinances, and commands" (Deut. 11:1).
- "Keep every command I am giving you today, so that you may have the strength to cross into and possess the land you are to inherit" (Deut. 11:8).
- "If you carefully obey My commands I am giving you today, to love the Lord your God and worship Him with all your heart and all your soul, I will provide rain for your land in season, the early and late rains, and you will harvest your grain, new wine, and oil. I will provide grass in your fields for your livestock. You will eat and be satisfied" (Deut. 11:13-15).
- "Look, today I set before you a blessing and a curse: there will be a blessing, if you obey the commands of the Lord your God I am giving you today, and a curse, if you do not obey the commands of the Lord your God, and you turn aside from the path I command you today by following other gods you have not known" (Deut. 11:26-28).

Jesus echoed this same obedience to the Father. "My sheep hear My voice," Jesus said. "I know them, and they follow Me" (John 10:27). They follow Me; this obedience to God's voice gives clear evidence of a covenant relationship. It is the key to covenant identity, usefulness, and enjoyment. To thrive in God's kingdom, we must obey His every word.

EK COMMUNITY Enlist an accountability partner, perhaps a member of your small group. Agree to encourage each other to remain obedient to God and His Word.

DAY 3
Covenant Keeper

If we were in a room together and I told you that there were two doors we could go through to exit the room, one door marked "Blessing" and the other "Cursing," I doubt either of us would rush to the door marked "Cursing." Yet this is what we do every time we disobey God's Word. We choose cursing over blessing. We choose death over life. We place ourselves in spiritual danger and render our lives ineffective in God's service. We lose sight of the kingdom.

This doesn't mean that our salvation is based on our performance. But it does mean that our obedience can directly impact God's blessing upon us. Our obedience also affects how useful we are to Him for His kingdom work.

God calls His people to be steadfast and faithful. If we couldn't be obedient to Him, He wouldn't expect it of us. If we couldn't do what He has said, He wouldn't have said it. Therefore, His "if–then" challenge should greet our ears with a note of encouragement.

Yes, we can keep His covenant.

Yes, we can be productive.

Yes, we can live as consistent kingdom citizens.

We know that God will keep His side of the bargain. And we are also sure that He will give us everything we need to hold up our side as well.

Maybe you have been disobedient, but His covenant still stands. This kingdom still calls to you. This God who promised blessing to the people of Israel stands beside you this very day keeping His promise—drawing you back into fellowship, offering you freedom in place of failure.

He wants you close. He wants you near him. He wants you to experience the fullness of the covenant every day. God has greater blessings in store for you. They hang in the balance of your obedience.

EK CHALLENGE Confess your disobedience to God and receive His full pardon. "If we confess our sins, He is faithful and righteous to forgive us our sins and to cleanse us from all unrighteousness" (1 John 1:9).

Birth of A Nation 4

In Exodus 19 the Israelites were referred to as the "house of Jacob," (v. 3). Their ancestor Jacob was a troublesome member of a troubled family. Jacob manipulated his twin brother to get his inheritance, then tricked their father to steal his brother's blessing. Jacob was later tricked in turn by his uncle who required Jacob to work seven years to get to marry his true love only to find after the wedding a different bride behind the veil.

Then Jacob wrestled all night with an angel, an experience that changed his life and his name. As the angel said to him at sunrise, " 'Your name will no longer be Jacob. ... It will be Israel because you have struggled with God and with men and have prevailed' " (Gen. 32:28).

Up until this point, the group of Jacob's descendants standing before God in Exodus 19 had only been known by their family name. They were of the "house of Jacob." Now they became the "sons of Israel." At this defining moment in their history, we witness in some ways the birth of the nation of Israel, God's people, a new day in their relationship with God.

This covenant community would no longer be known just for where they had come from. They would now be known for who they were—the people of God, His own unique possession created to carry out a crucial role in reaching the nations and to fulfill God's kingdom purposes.

The statement from the last part of Exodus 19:5 confirms this fact. When God said, " 'You will be My own possession out of all the peoples, although all the earth is Mine,' " He was not simply affirming His ownership of the physical earth, His rightful claim as Creator. He was also using this phrase to describe His relationship with Israel—not to give them privilege and standing alone but to give them purpose. They were to be His possession, not to be admired on a shelf but to be maneuvered full force into the world.

Attempt today to serve God as His movable possession, seeing the world through His eyes of love wherever you go.

SEEK LOVE

DAY 5
How Movable Are You?

About 12 years ago God picked me up in Norfolk, Virginia, where I was pastor of a great church and set me down in Atlanta, Georgia, where I served the Southern Baptist Convention as a church growth specialist. We built our dream house there. Two years after that God moved us to Texas where I served as president of Southwestern Seminary. Nine years later I found myself at home, just outside Nashville, Tennessee, typing this manuscript.

Looking back over the last 12 years, God seems to have said to us, "You can build your dream home and make all the plans you want to make, but always remember that you are a movable treasure."

You may be thinking, *Guys like you are supposed to do that, Ken. You're a preacher. Ministers are always being called to other assignments.* Maybe so. But look back at Exodus 19:5. It wasn't just Moses and the other leaders of Israel that God claimed as His movable possessions. He summoned the whole nation to this privileged calling. We are all God's precious, movable possessions. God has a purpose for each one of us wherever He places us.

This gives new meaning, then, to what we should be thinking about as we're standing in line at the supermarket, waiting in the dentist's office, or shooting the breeze after a game of tennis. In any or all of these places—and countless others—God may have moved us there with a distinct purpose far beyond what we were expecting.

Perhaps when stuck in line at the store, you can strike up a conversation with the person behind you, injecting a simple note of God's reality in the midst of a how-are-you-doing moment. Perhaps you can spend a few minutes in the waiting room encouraging someone who's sitting near you rather than wasting your time reading last year's magazines. Who knows? God may have placed you there for a kingdom moment to embody His name, to embrace His mission.

To prepare for your next small-group session, read Exodus 19:1-5. Think about how these verses apply to you.

**EK
KNOWLEDGE**

Highly Prized

Let's look a little deeper at what it means to be God's possession. Some translations of the Bible render "My own possession" (Ex. 19:5) as "My peculiar people," which comes from a Latin word for "property." We are indeed a rather peculiar lot, aren't we? Yet with all of our peculiarities, God still calls us his own special treasure.

Some commentators have even linked this wording to a term referring to a personal collection or hoard. The idea of a "peculiar" treasure, then—when seen in this light—is of a unique and exclusive possession among all the others. God's people are like this to Him—His crown jewel, His masterwork, His one of a kind.[1] And He never wanted Israel to forget it:

- "You are a holy people belonging to the Lord your God. The Lord your God has chosen you to be His own possession out of all the peoples on the face of the earth" (Deut. 7:6; 14:2).
- "Today the Lord has affirmed that you are His special people as He promised you, that you are to keep all His commands" (Deut. 26:18).
- " 'They will be Mine,' says the Lord of Hosts. 'a special possession on the day I am preparing. I will have compassion on them as a man has compassion on his son who serves him' " (Mal. 3:17).

A loving father takes his child's face in his hands, looks deeply into her eyes, and affirms over and over that "you are my special child." It boggles my mind to think that the sovereign God of the universe, the Creator of all that exists, has chosen to take His children into His arms and declare: "You are special to me." But this is the unquestionable reality of what the Bible teaches us. We are God's people by His own gracious choice. We are His most most highly valuable possessions.

Read these verses again. Rewrite them to make them personal, using your own name.

EK TRUTH   [1]John I. Durham, "Exodus," *Word Bible Commentary* (Waco: Word Books, 1987), 262.

7

A King and His People

When you become a kingdom person, you belong to God.

In 2003, we moved from the president's home at Southwestern Baptist Seminary in Texas to a condominium in Tennessee. We knew we wouldn't have room for all our possessions. But the move wasn't just about stuff. It was about moving our lives and about our belief that we had a kingdom purpose for moving.

Exodus tells the the story of God moving His people out of slavery and how God began to teach them their kingdom purpose. This is where we will begin exploring what the Bible teaches us about the kingdom of God. The first mention of the kingdom in the Bible is found in a pivotal passage from Exodus 19:6.

EK COMMUNITY

1. When you move, what are some things you can take? What must be left behind?

2. If you had to move, what are some treasured possessions you would have to take with you to your new home?

◆ Use the corresponding *EKG* DVD segment for this session now.

> God had been building and uniting His people from the beginning of time through the entire account of Genesis, the first book or the Bible. Their story continued through God's dealings with their forefathers Abraham, Isaac, Jacob, and Joseph; through Israel's descent into slavery in Egypt; and through the miraculous deliverance of His people from Pharaoh's control.
>
> At the beginning of Exodus 19 it had been three months to the day since the liberating miracle that started their move

EK TRUTH

The Israelites were in the rough, rocky, empty region of Sinai. They had been brought here on the wings of a promise—a promise made in an audible voice by God to Moses from the unburned branches of the burning bush: "This will be the sign to you that I have sent you: when you bring the people out of Egypt, you will all worship God at this mountain" (Ex. 3:12).

1. What was supernatural about how the Israelites went from slavery to camping in the desert three months later?

2. In God's message in Exodus 19:1-6, underline what God told Moses to say to the Israelites. What would you do next if these things were said to you?

3. How were Abraham and his descendants, the Israelites, examples of being God's movable possessions?

4. Name some current examples of kingdom people who are God's movable possessions.

> **Read Exodus 19:1-6.**
> *In the third month, on the same day [of the month] that the Israelites had left the land of Egypt, they entered the Wilderness of Sinai. After they departed from Rephidim, they entered the Wilderness of Sinai and camped in the wilderness, and Israel camped there in front of the mountain.*
>
> *Moses went up the mountain to God, and the LORD called to him from the mountain: "This is what you must say to the house of Jacob, and explain to the Israelites: You have seen what I did to the Egyptians and how I carried you on eagles' wings and brought you to Me. Now if you will listen to Me and carefully keep My covenant, you will be My own possession out of all the peoples, although all the earth is Mine, and you will be My kingdom of priests and My holy nation. These are the words that you are to say to the Israelites."*

5. How would people called "God's holy nation" have to be different?

This week as part of God's holy nation, explain how you will do the following:

EK LOVE

• worship God;

• share the good news of salvation;

• minister to the hurting;

• make God's love real to the world.

Write specific ways to

• embrace His mission;

• embody His name;

• obey His Word.

> **God Wants You!**
> This was no distant, impersonal deity speaking. This was God, who is love, who had redeemed His people and cared for their every need. He not only wanted them safe; He wanted them with Him.
>
> It was probably difficult for the children of Israel to believe that the God of creation, God, who had sustained Abraham, Isaac, and Jacob, and who now spoke to Moses on the mountaintop, truly desired to have a personal relationship with them, a covenant relationship. But He did.
>
> And He still wants a personal relationship with His people today!

Share briefly in your group what you will be doing in the week ahead. Pray that each person in your group will be God's movable possession, serving as His priest wherever he or she goes throughout the week.

EK PRAYER

THE NATURE OF COVENANT

A covenant is a binding pact, treaty, or agreement between two parties. There are many examples of covenants. The marriage relationship is a covenant between a man and a woman and made before God and witnesses. In the Bible, Jonathan and David formed a covenant of friendship. The prophets condemned Israel for covenants God's people made with ungodly nations. God was under no obligation to enter into a covenant relationship with Israel, yet He chose to do so. This is a huge—a major—consistent theme throughout the Bible.

EK
KNOWLEDGE

A covenant is a type of promise, or contract. God chose to bring His people into a covenant relationship with Himself.

• Identify a covenant you have made.

• How has your promise shaped your life?

• If you have a covenant relationship with someone, describe it briefly.

• In the next chapter of Exodus, God gave His people the Ten Commandments. How are those Commandments part of our covenant relationship with God?

GOD'S COVENANTS

When Noah and his family emerged from the ark, God promised never to repeat a flood of global proportions (Gen. 9:9–17). He confirmed this covenant with a rainbow. In this case the covenant God made required no human response. It was a solemn commitment to humanity on the part of holy God.

God also made a covenant with Abraham (Gen. 12:1-3; 15:18). God told Abraham to leave his family and go out to the land He would show him. God promised that Abraham's descendants would be a blessing to all nations.

Yet, three months after Israel's deliverance from Egypt, God told His people that this unique and profound, relationship between the two of them would no longer be as simple. From this day forward it would be a relationship that would grow or weaken, based on how His people kept the covenant.

> "In one Gallup survey, we discovered, on the basis of a twelve-item scale, that only 13 percent of Americans have what might be called a truly transforming faith." The point is clear, our profession of faith does not always translate into transformed lifestyle."
> —George Gallup Jr. and Tim Jones, *The Saints Among Us*
>
> How can a focus on God's kingdom transform your faith and your life?

"Now if you will listen to Me and carefully keep My covenant, you will be My own possession out of all the peoples, although all the earth is Mine, and you will be My kingdom of priests and My holy nation. These are the words you are to say to the Israelites" *(Exodus 19:5-6).*

As you process the upcoming devotions and prepare for the next session, for a more complete study, read Section 2, "A King and His Purpose," in *Empowering Kingdom Growth: The Heartbeat of God* (Nashville: Broadman & Holman, 2004).

- Reflect on Exodus 19:5-6. Discuss these key points of God's promise.

EK TRUTH

1. God never threatened to send His people back to Egypt. They had already been rescued by His act of redemptive grace. The obedience prescribed in the covenant would all occur after redemption had already taken place. In the same way, we do not earn or buy our salvation by any work of obedience on our part.

2. God did not force Israel to serve Him the way a conquering king might have been expected to do. This is a key for understanding the nature of our King and what it means to be a kingdom person. We are not forced to obey. We are invited to love. And in love He warns us that our disobedience will cause us unnecessary harm and suffering.

3. Obedience was not a condition of deliverance, but a doorway to its fullness. This was obedience motivated by thankfulness for what God had done. It enabled the people to enjoy both their relationship with God and their usefulness in His purpose, to experience everything their redemption had won for them.

Explain this statement: Obedience is inseparable from covenant.

EK CHALLENGE

Sermon Notes / **A King and His People**

Scripture Text

Main Points
1.

2.

3.

Meaningful Illustrations

Personal Application

DAY 8 Living Sacrifices

We—the people of God, His prized and movable treasures—are the "living sacrifices" God uses to advance His kingdom on earth. But what kinds of "living sacrifices" does a kingdom person make to God?

Our bodies—"Therefore, brothers, by the mercies of God, I urge you to present your bodies as a living sacrifice, holy and pleasing to God; this is your spiritual worship" (Rom. 12:1). By continuing to read though Romans 12, we discover the Apostle Paul is not only talking about the purity of our personal bodies but also the united sacrifices made by the body of believers, the church. By offering back to Him all the physical abilities and spiritual gifts He has given to us—as individuals and as churches—we fulfill a major part of our priestly duties.

Our worship—"Therefore, through Him let us continually offer up to God a sacrifice of praise, that is, the fruit of our lips that confess His name" (Heb. 13:15). Have you ever thought about worship as being a priestly sacrifice you can offer to God? This perspective should arrest our attention the next time we approach worship halfheartedly. True worship occurs when we focus on God as the object of our praise and adoration.

Our service—"Don't neglect to do good and to share, for God is pleased with such sacrifices" (Heb. 13:16). By actively planning to be thoughtful, watchful, caring, and compassionate, we meet the needs of those around us and please our Father at the same time.

Our witness—Paul talked about being a "priest of God's good news," with his purpose being that "the offering of the Gentiles may be acceptable" as a result of receiving God's salvation (Rom. 15:16). He saw his sharing of the gospel message as a stewardship, an act of priestly service and obedience, a way to help others experience the joy of Christ's presence and acceptance.

Worship, service, witness—three ways to love God and love others. You can show your love for God this week by worshiping Him and being His movable possession as you tell others about God's love.

EK LOVE

Serving Others
9 DAY

Serving is at the heart of the priestly role. Through poetic prophecy Isaiah challenged Israel to take on the priestly role they were called to embody. We, too, can learn from what he said: "The Spirit of the Lord GOD is on Me, because the LORD has anointed Me to bring good news to the poor. He has sent Me to heal the brokenhearted, to proclaim liberty to the captives, and freedom to the prisoners" (Isa. 61:1).

Jesus Christ read from this text at the synagogue in Nazareth and declared, " 'Today as you listen, this Scripture has been fulfilled' " (Luke 4:21). As followers of Christ , these same ministries are also our priestly calling: to share the good news of salvation, to minister to the hurting, to make God's love real to the world.

The prophet Isaiah was speaking to Israel when he reminded them, "You will be called the LORD's priests; they will speak of you as ministers of our God" (Isa. 61:6). Isaiah emphasized the role they should play and the name by which they should be known.

Isaiah also prophesied about the good news of salvation being meant for more than the nation of Israel. As Isaiah gave God's message concerning Jesus and the fulfillment of this priestly prophecy, he said, "It is not enough for you to be My servant raising up the tribes of Jacob and restoring the protected ones of Israel. I will also make you a light for the nations, to be My salvation to the ends of the earth" (Isa. 49:6).

To be God's priests is a calling for all of us, a calling for us to serve all people, to the ends of the earth.

Serving others is how we obey God's Word, embrace His mission, and embody His name—the role of a priest. How does this truth apply to you as a kingdom person?

EK TRUTH

DAY 10 Holiness

Many writers have offered numerous suggestions on how we can achieve purity of heart and soul. Some people read these books looking for a simple formula, hoping to find a low-commitment path to holiness.

It's kind of like dieting. The experts lead us from fad to fad, creating as many side effects as they do success stories. But it basically boils down to this: to lose weight, eat less and exercise more. It's a fairly simple formula.

For those who are looking for simple steps to holiness, I'll give you just one: we experience holiness by being obedient to the Lord. This is because partial obedience is total disobedience. Delayed obedience is present-tense disobedience. Thus, full obedience is the only cure for disobedience.

I know that many people today—many Christians, in fact—do not live consistently by the teachings of God's Word. Truth is, we all face a daily struggle to let His truth capture our affections and control our behavior. But obedience is the only proper response for a kingdom person.

Why obey? Because He has redeemed us. "For the grace of God has appeared, with salvation for all people, instructing us to deny godlessness and worldly lusts and to live in a sensible, righteous, and godly way in the present age" (Titus 2:11-12).

Why obey? Because He is holy. "As the One who called you is holy, you also are to be holy in all your conduct; for it is written, 'Be holy, because I am holy'" (1 Pet. 1:15-16).

Why obey? Because this is His purpose for us. "Look, today I set before you a blessing and a curse: [there will be] a blessing, if you obey the commands of the Lord your God I am giving you today" (Deut. 11:26-27).

Obedience opens the floodgate for blessing, which enables us to be a blessing to others.

To become holy, how can you change? Create your own spiritual fitness program to feed on God's Word and exercise your witness.

EK CHALLENGE

One Eternal Name

This name we bear is the only name that will last forever. That's why we cannot talk about God's name without a final glimpse at the promise of an eternal kingdom. When the Lord told David that he would establish the work of Solomon's hands in building the temple, he went on to say that he would " 'appoint him over My house and My kingdom forever, and his throne will be established forever' " (1 Chron. 17:14).

We know now that the Lord's reference to "forever" in His message to David found its ultimate fulfillment in Jesus, the Son of David ... who was born in Bethlehem, the city of David ... and who lives forever on the throne of his Father's kingdom. We, too, will live with him forever.

Still, we may long to see in our lifetime the fulfillment of all the things God has started in us. But neither we nor God's kingdom are limited to a human lifetime. Because we will walk on streets of gold and live forever in the glory of God's eternal kingdom, we can live free from the restraints of now and next week.

Yes, those of us who embody His name today can already enjoy a taste of His eternal kingdom. We live and serve and work and play in a kingdom that has no boundaries, no restrictions, no limits, and no end. This joyful task of embodying God's name places us squarely in the middle of God's will for this hour and forever in the freedom of His purposes for eternity.

Someone may ask you, "How can you be nice to that guy after he's been so awful to you?" or, "How are you able to be so patient with your children?" or, "Why does your family seem so happy and connected?" If they do, tell them there's a name for what they see in you.

His name is Jesus.

Part of the joy of eternity with God is being with those we love. Whom do you look forward to seeing in heaven? What can you do this week to encourage those who are not yet kingdom people to make heaven their eternal home?

EK KNOWLEDGE

DAY 12 God's Stamp

Soon after the dedication of the magnificent temple in Jerusalem, the Queen of Sheba traveled 1,500 miles from the Persian Gulf region, her camel caravan loaded down with spices and precious gifts. She came partly because she had heard of the wisdom of Solomon. But she had come for more of a reason than that! "The queen of Sheba heard about Solomon's fame connected with the name of the LORD and came to test him with difficult questions" (1 Kings 10:1).

The temple was impressive. Solomon's splendor was immense. But the thing that turned the head of the queen was the indelible stamp of God on the life of one of His people. That's why, after sufficiently picking his brain, she concluded that the rumors she had heard about Solomon's brilliance didn't tell half the story. This pagan queen recognized God's blessing in Solomon's life, saying, "He delighted in you and put you on the throne of Israel, because of the LORD's eternal love for Israel. He has made you king to carry out justice and righteousness" (v. 9).

God's name is visible in His people, even from a distance. We continue to see throughout the Scripture the weaving together of three threads:

1. God called a people to embrace His mission—to be His chosen instruments in drawing the nations to Himself.
2. He established a covenant relationship with them so they would embody His name and represent His nature and character to the world.
3. He commanded that they obey His Word and demonstrate holiness, the noticeable difference He made in their lives.

You can be a welcoming reminder that God is waiting for those tired of slogging through a world of sin and disappointments. Let them see God's light in your window. It may seem as impressive as Solomon's temple.

Pray that God's indelible stamp on your life will be visible to all as you seek to make His name great.

EK PRAYER

God's Glory
13 DAY

When God acts in human history, it is always for our good and His glory. Lest you wonder which one of these is the more important of the two, God's glory always comes first.

For example, when God began to move on behalf of His people being held captive in Babylon, He made clear through the prophet Ezekiel that " 'it is not for your sake that I will act, house of Israel, but for My holy name, which you profaned among the nations where you went' " (Ezek. 36:22).

Their deliverance was about God's desire that the nations see and come to know Him as the living God. Everything is about God, and His kingdom people must embrace His mission as their own.

Like Israel, we are tempted to think that we are the center of the universe, that our desires and prayers determine God's agenda. Part of me wishes this were true. This kind of message has an immediate appeal.. But when I consider the end result of this kind of theology—the self-centered emptiness of expecting God to bow to our personal wishes—I don't want any part of what it offers. It's like peeling away the layers of an onion, working our way further down into ourselves until there's nothing left to show for all of our struggle.

When we pray that God will be glorified, He will send us deliverance, or faithfulness, patience, strength, courage, wisdom–whatever is required to reveal His presence and draw others to Him. The sooner we understand that God is King—that He alone is the center of the universe—the sooner we'll come to experience the freedom of living in His kind of purpose and protection. It is indeed the only way to live.

EK KNOWLEDGE

Do you have self-serving layers you need to strip away to see that God is King and the center of the universe? Applying what you have read this week and preparing for the next small group session, think about the ways you embody God's name, making His name—not your own—the driving force behind all you do.

14 A King and His Purpose

To redeem a people for Himself, to make a name for Himself.

Alexander the Great was in a fierce battle when he saw one of his soldiers flee in fear. Normally this offense would have been punishable by immediate death. The soldier, hardly more than a boy, was brought before the conqueror. When asked his name, the young man answered, "Alexander."

Those watching this encounter noted that Alexander the Great softened upon hearing the soldier's name was the same as his own. He spared the man's life with these words, "Change your name or change your behavior!"

• Growing up what did it mean to you to have your name(s)?

EK COMMUNITY

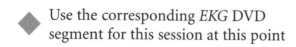 Use the corresponding *EKG* DVD segment for this session at this point

There was nothing all that special about this one nation. Others were bigger and more powerful. But God had redeemed Israel from Pharaoh's whip, not just to show them mercy but to "make a name for Himself." Their covenant relationship with God distinguished them from all other peoples in the world.

> **God's People**
> *"Who is like Your people Israel? God came to one nation on earth in order to redeem a people for Himself, to make a name for Himself, and to perform for them great and awesome acts, driving out nations and their gods before Your people You redeemed for Yourself from Egypt"*
> (2 Sam. 7:23)

The importance and significance of this fact had never been lost on David, who prayed that God would do what He had promised concerning the temple and the kingly line, "so that Your name will be exalted forever, when it is said, " 'The LORD of Hosts is God over Israel' " (2 Sam. 7:26).

God's kingdom, embodying God's name, is all that matters. Surely this is what the psalmist meant when he sang, "Not to us, LORD, not to us, but to Your name give glory because of Your faithful love, because of Your truth. Why should the nations say, 'Where is their God?'" (Ps. 115:1-2).

Yes, there is joy and strength and lasting purpose in embodying the name of the Lord.

1. How can God's people make God's name great?

EK TRUTH   • Do you think most Christians …

❑ act as if they are ashamed of God's name;
❑ do nothing to make His name great;
❑ represent God, make His name great, and draw people to Him.

Which of these describes you best? Why?

• How could you make His name great?

2. "The LORD will not abandon His people, because of His great name and because He has determined to make you His own people" (1 Sam. 12:22). What did God's name mean to the Israelites?

> **God's Character**
> God's name stands for His character. He reveals His name, in its many different forms and aspects, as a way of inviting His people to live with Him in a dynamic, intimate relationship.
> Which characteristics of God are most important to you? How can you embody that aspect of God in order to reveal that image of God and make His name great?

- When we are born we inherit a name. With it comes a reputation to live up to or to try to change. The name we bear as kingdom citizens is the only name that will last forever. As we embody or represent God's name, individually and collectively, what is our contribution to the eternal name we share as His people?

- What could be some practical (or impractical!) results of embodying God's name for His glory?

- How does knowing that you are representing God's name for this and future generations affect your commitment to make His name great?

- How have some media images and stories today helped God's name?

- How have some media images and stories today hurt God's name?

> **In God's Name, We . . .**
> A recent survey conducted by the Barna Research Group reported that 65 percent of Americans are concerned about the future, with roughly 74 percent of those citing moral decay in America and the world as their primary concern. (Source: Baptist Press)
>
> If Christians seek to embody God's name and make His name great, what impact could their witness have upon moral decay and the future?

- How have media images affected the way you embody God's name?

- How can the promise of eternity with Jesus free you to embody God's name each day?

3. Read Solomon's Prayer.
When Solomon prayed at the temple dedication ceremony, he left us with a charge that still rings in our ears.

You see, this building was designed for more than Israel's worship needs. God wanted to reach the non-Israelites, the foreigners, anyone who did not know Him. In fact, every blessing God bestows on His people—including this house of prayer and worship—is intended to have a global, eternal impact.

The modern-day parallels this passage brings to mind are too great for me to pass up. When we have a desire to build a new church building or to add to our existing structure, do we plan and build with the "foreigner" in mind?

> **Solomon's Prayer**
> *"Even for the foreigner who is not of Your people Israel but has come from a distant land because of Your name—for they will hear of Your great name, mighty hand, and outstretched arm, and will come and pray toward this temple—may You hear in heaven, Your dwelling place, and do according to all the foreigner asks You for. Then all the people on earth will know Your name, to fear You as Your people Israel do and know that this temple I have built is called by Your name"* (1 Kings 8:41-43).

• How does your church—both in the use of its building and in other activities—provide for those people who do not claim the name of Christ, "foreigners," who are not yet kingdom citizens?

Naturally, this doesn't mean that our churches should woo visitors at the expense of worshiping God. Yet, drawing people is one of God's specified purposes for the house where His name dwells. Should we not ask, "What impact will this new facility have on our ability to reach the unsaved? Are our plans for this expansion the highest and best use of God's resources as He implements His kingdom plans through us?"

• What are some dreams or visions group members have of personal ministries or church ministries—actions they or the church can do to make God's name great?

EK CHALLENGE

How would you like your name to be known and remembered? How does part of that desired legacy embody the name of God?

As you read this week's devotionals and prepare for the next small-group session, for a more complete study, read Section 3, "His Kingdom Comes," in *Empowering Kingdom Growth: The Heartbeat of God* (Nashville: Broadman & Holman, 2004).

EK LOVE

David wrote in Psalm 103:1, "My soul, praise the LORD, and all that is within me, praise His holy name." In your devotion and actions this week, how will you embody your love and praise to God?

EK PRAYER

This week how will you take God's name to those who do not know Him? Share with one another names of people you encounter throughout the week who are not Christians.

EK KNOWLEDGE

GOD ACTS "FOR HIS NAME'S SAKE"

God acts in a manner consistent with His nature and character. This is something He declares many times throughout the Bible. When God leads us in paths of righteousness (Ps. 23:3), forgives our sins (Ps. 25:11), guides us through the snares and seductions of life (Ps. 31:3), delivers us from our sins (Ps. 79:9), deals kindly with us (Ps. 109:21), and, indeed, lets us live at all (Ps. 143:11), He does these things "for His name's sake."

GOD IN US, NOT IN "IT"

Some commentators suggest that the splendor of the temple itself would draw the foreigner in God's direction. No doubt, some of the Israelites may have shared this idea. But Solomon's prayer at the temple dedication captured the true intent of God's vision, that the foreigner "will hear of [His] great name, mighty hand, and outstretched arm, and will come and pray toward this temple" (1 Kings 8:42). God's name was the initial draw; the temple was merely the destination for their response.

Sermon Notes / **A King and His Purpose**

Scripture Text

Main Points

1.

2.

3.

Meaningful Illustrations

Personal Application

DAY 15

Hope for Renewal

In the midst of crisis, with Israel at its lowest ebb, Ezekiel declared God's intention to revive His people, to rally His kingdom. Many years before, of course, God had redeemed Israel from Egypt. And by His transforming power, they had emerged not as a loose collection of families but as a nation, a kingdom of priests. And He was about to do it again.

The long night in Babylon would mark another turning point in the life of Israel. They had been taken into captivity a proud nation, but they would emerge as a new spiritual entity, a revitalized remnant that would return home with a new and responsive heart, a transformed people who would possess God's Spirit within them.

What we are witnessing here is the forerunner of the New Testament church, God's messianic community. We are witnessing God's kingdom rousing from the appearance of sleep, yet marching (as always) to the beat of God's sovereign purpose and perfect timing. We are witnessing what happens when God revives us from our rebellion.

Revival always begins with a righteous remnant. We see this truth coming to vivid life in the prophecy of Ezekiel, through words and phrases that still have the power to renew our troubled souls. When we hear Ezekiel speaking to the people of Israel (Ezek. 36:24-38), promising them God's cleansing, His renewal, His empowerment, and His restoration to fruitful ministry, we can feel our own sins falling away, the tug of temptation loosening its grip, and our spirits taking deep breaths of hope, vision, and freshness.

This is the kingdom. This is the power of God rushing through our veins, restoring our weak and damaged arteries, performing His sovereign act of revival so that His kingdom work can pour forth through us in power.

Take a moment to let the truth of God's forgiveness penetrate your soul. Whatever your sin, God's promise is that you can be clean and a vital part of His kingdom.

EK TRUTH

Cleansing

It's not enough for us to be rescued from our sins, to be pulled from harm's way and returned to safety. We must also be renewed.

The promise of restoration comes hand in hand with a moral and spiritual change of heart. So God told His people Israel that they must be purified from the filthy buildup caused by their rebellion and idolatry. Ezekiel used the terminology of sprinkling with clean water (Ezek. 36:25), a reference to a temple ritual that symbolized washing spiritual uncleanness from the people. But this sprinkling is much more than a lick and a promise we give ourselves. This is something only God can do, a deep cleansing action that sets us free from the guilt our disobedience has caused.

God's demands for holiness and purity have not changed since Ezekiel spoke these words. If we desire restoration today in our own lives and churches, we also must allow the Father to cleanse us from our filthiness.

Study after study has indicated that the lifestyles chosen by many of us who claim to be Christians are so much like those of the world, our witness is being dulled by the compromise. We are desperately in need of this cleansing of our hearts and minds. The formula has never changed: we must turn from our wickedness in true humility and allow God's Word to purify us. Just as Jesus asked the Father to sanctify the disciples with the truth of His Word (John 17:17), we too must seek the deep cleansing of God—if we are serious about being kingdom people.

Do you know someone who carries a load of guilt? Share God's message of forgiveness and cleansing today.

EK COMMUNITY

DAY 17 A New Heart

When God brings restoration, He doesn't stop with the cleansing part. He doesn't just remove our sin; He also heals and revives. He performs radical surgery on us, enabling His people to live in obedience to His Word. He gives us a "new heart" removing our "heart of stone" and giving us a "heart of flesh" (Ezek. 36:26)—a heart that's alive and healthy and thriving.

The heart is not just one individual part of a person's makeup. It represents our total personality. We use the term *heart* to refer to our mind, will, and emotions. In the Bible it stands for the seat of our personality.

Jesus, you may remember, called the scribes and Pharisees " 'hypocrites' " because they honored Him with their lips " 'but their heart is far from Me' " (Matt. 15:7-8, quoting Isa. 29:13). These men, unrivaled in their obsession with ceremonial purity, were greatly offended. Christ's disciples, too, appeared somewhat shocked by His implication. Didn't Jesus know that these men had every appearance of holiness and uprightness? Yes, but Jesus knew more. He knew their " 'evil thoughts, murders, adulteries, sexual immoralities, thefts, false testimonies, blasphemies' " (Matt. 15:19) and all the rest, and He knew from where these secret sins came. "From the heart" come the things that define a person. Our hearts tell us who we really are.

Israel's heart had become fossilized, like a stone, unfeeling and unresponsive. But God promised to do for them what they could not do for themselves. He would give them a heart of flesh, a heart He could mold and move and fashion, a heart that could hear His Word and react in obedience.

EK KNOWLEDGE

Psalm 139 begins: "Lord, You have searched me and known me. You know when I sit down and when I stand up; You understand my thoughts from far away. You observe my travels and my rest; You are aware of all my ways. Before a word is on my tongue, You know all about it, Lord." The psalm ends, "Search me, God, and know my heart; test me and know my concerns. See if there is any offensive way in me; lead me in the everlasting way." When God looks at your heart, what does He see?

A New Spirit

Not only was Israel set to receive a new heart, but God also promised, "I will place My Spirit within you." God's Spirit would enable them "to follow My statutes and carefully observe My ordinances" (Ezek. 36:27).

The promises of God's covenant had been based on Israel's obedience to His Word. But their struggle to obey the law demonstrated that the human heart is wicked. In our own strength we cannot keep God's law. We need our hearts reset, restored, and revived. We need God's life inside of us, His eternal Holy Spirit. There's no other way to live the kingdom life. Kingdom people don't pull themselves up by their own bootstraps. They submit to God and give God's power a clear, obedient path. Jeremiah described this:

" 'This is the covenant I will make with the house of Israel after those days'—the Lord's declaration. 'I will place My law within them and write it on their hearts. I will be their God, and they will be My people. No longer will one teach his neighbor or his brother, saying: Know the Lord, for they will all know Me, from the least to the greatest of them'—the Lord's declaration. 'For I will forgive their wrongdoing and never again remember their sin' " *(Jer. 31:33-34).*

We are the recipients of this new covenant. These prophetic Scriptures were a sign that a new age was dawning, a time when God would "pour water on the thirsty land, and streams on the dry ground [and] pour out My Spirit on your descendants and My blessing on your offspring" (Isa. 44:3). It foretold of a coming One who would have "My Spirit on Him" (Isa. 42:1) and would empower the people of His kingdom to obey His Word and experience His full blessing. The world was preparing for Jesus. The kingdom was coming in force!

Thank God for the presence of His Holy Spirit in your life today. Pray for His ongoing guidance to help you to obey His Word and experience His blessings.

EK PRAYER

DAY 19 Kingdom Invasion

Jesus' message was not like anything these early disciples had ever heard. Everyone was saying so: "When Jesus had finished this sermon, the crowds were astonished at His teaching, because He was teaching them like one who had authority, and not like their scribes" (Matt. 7:28-29). He promised that God's rule and reign were invading planet Earth through His own ministry. A passion for His righteousness would penetrate their very lives, and they in turn would spread the news of this kingdom, becoming fishers of men.

Jesus was not simply inviting them to become recipients of the kingdom. He was empowering them to become agents of the kingdom, giving them the joy of encouraging others to experience this blessing, now and forever.

Yes, even to this very day, God promises blessing—not to the strong, the powerful, and the mighty but to the poor in spirit, to those who mourn, who are gentle, who hunger for His righteousness, who are merciful and pure in heart, and who seek peace even when it's returned as persecution.

And how does God bless them?

He declares, " 'The kingdom of heaven is theirs.' "

They shall be comforted. They shall inherit the earth, enjoying kingdom benefits even on this side of heaven. They shall be satisfied in their quest for righteousness. They shall be shown the indescribable mercy of being called the sons and daughters of God. They will not always be spared the sting of suffering, but they will receive the eternal reward of their Father. They enjoy the blessing of God, a constant relationship with the King of glory (Matt.5:3-10).

And isn't that blessing enough?

Does your heart swell with gratitude at God's forgiveness and blessings in your life? Express your love to God by sharing His love with someone who has not yet experienced the gift of salvation. God will thank you.

EK LOVE

Times of Temptation

After Jesus had fasted forty days and nights in the wilderness—a reminder of the forty years Israel had spent in the wilderness (Deut. 8:2-3)—Satan came to Him. (This is typical. Satan always approaches us when he thinks we're at our weakest.) The first temptation struck hard at Jesus' immediate needs: loneliness, hunger, and credibility (Matt.4:1-11).

All alone out here, Jesus? What kind of father leaves his son all by himself in the middle of nowhere with nothing to eat?

Hungry, Jesus? Surely for a miracle worker like You, these little loaf-sized stones are only bread in disguise.

You're the Son of God, Jesus? I might believe it myself if you'd prove it to me.

Jesus responded by quoting from Deuteronomy 8:3: "He humbled you by letting you go hungry; then He gave you manna to eat, which you and your fathers had not known, so that you might learn that man does not live on bread alone but on every word that comes from the mouth of the LORD." Jesus knew what Israel had failed to comprehend—that we, God's people, can rely on the Father for our every need. But we have to put first things first.

Jesus' first desire was unquestioned obedience to the Father's plan for His life. Thus He would do nothing—absolutely nothing—that would compromise their relationship. This "first things first" reality is what Jesus would later teach His disciples, telling them to " 'seek first the kingdom' " and trust God to provide all they needed (Matt. 6:33). When we tend first to our spiritual needs, God takes care of our physical needs without our even having to think about them.

EK CHALLENGE

When does temptation come to you? When you are hungry, lonely, afraid? Reflect on your temptations and the events and emotions surrounding those times. Ask God to help you through such difficulties in the future so that you can put first things first and focus on the kingdom.

21

His Kingdom Comes

The kingdom offers the promise of hope and renewal.

If you're a football fan, you've undoubtedly seen a play develop that was an absolute disconnect. The quarterback expected his receiver to break for the end zone, but instead he pulled up short. The pass, timed to hit the receiver in stride, sailed far over his head, incomplete—or worse, intercepted. Because of the receiver's lack of understanding or poor execution, the result was a failed play.

EK COMMUNITY

- Compare your life to a football game. Has there been a time when you went out for a pass, a life opportunity, only to find too late you went too far, or the wrong direction. Sometimes life just hasn't worked out the way you planned. What happened? How did you feel?

- Can you recall a time when your life took a direction that resulted in a disconnect from God? What happened?

Falling captive to the Babylon empire had left the once-proud people struggling for survival. Their vital signs weakened during the long, lonely, exile that followed. They realized too late the penalty for ignoring the prophets who diagnosed their heart condition. Israel knew they had disobeyed God. Meanwhile their hearts had been turning to stone. Their national upheaval, their loss of freedom—their spiritual heart attack—were the result of years of rebellion.

EK TRUTH

1. Sin has consequences, and not just for us.

  • True or false: If I choose to _____, no one but me will ever know.

  • True or false: So what if I use _____? It doesn't hurt anyone but me.

• True or false: I'm pretty good. I don't do anything wrong. I go to church, so I'm a good Christian, right?

• Who is hurt when God does not have rule and reign in His people's lives?

• Who is hurt when people sin?

2. Read Ezekiel 36:22-23.
"Therefore, say to the house of Israel: This is what the Lord GOD says: It is not for your sake that I will act, house of Israel, but for My holy name, which you profaned among the nations where you went. I will honor the holiness of My great name, which has been profaned among the nations—the name you have profaned among them. The nations will know that I am Yahweh"—the declaration of the Lord GOD—"when I demonstrate My holiness through you in their sight."

• According to this passage, who is ultimately hurt when God's people sin and profane His name?

• Why did God restore the people of Israel?

His name –

3. God's kingdom offers hope and renewal. **Read Ezekiel 36:25-29,32,36,38.**

"I will also sprinkle clean water on you, and you will be clean. I will cleanse you from all your impurities and all your idols. I will give you a new heart and put a new spirit within you; I will remove your heart of stone and give you a heart of flesh. I will place My Spirit within you and cause you to follow My statutes and carefully observe My ordinances. Then you will live in the land that I gave your fathers; you will be My people, and I will be your God. I will save you from all your uncleanness. ... It is not for your sake that I will act. ... Then the nations that remain around you will know that I, the LORD, have rebuilt what was destroyed and have replanted what was desolate. ... Then they will know that I am the LORD."

• Has sin ever hardened your heart, made it like stone? Did your repentance lead to God's cleansing? Describe the feeling when God gave you a new heart, a heart of flesh.

• Who saw God's power when the people of Israel were restored in their relationship to God?

• Who sees God's power today when people turn from sin to God?

• In which phrases of Ezekiel 36 can you see God's desire that kingdom people embody God's name, embrace His mission, and obey His Word?

Embody _____

Embrace _____

Obey_____

4. Read Matthew 3:1-2.

• When a person comes near the kingdom of God, what is the proper response? Why?

> In those days John the Baptist came, preaching in the Wilderness of Judea and saying, "Repent, because the kingdom of heaven has come near!" (Matt. 3:1-2).

In Matthew 3, John the Baptist had been preaching to the crowds in the wilderness. He was announcing that Jesus, the promised Messiah, would soon be revealed and that "the kingdom of heaven has come near."

• In God's kingdom today, as in John's time, what role does repentance have in God's rule and reign?

EK CHALLENGE Do you sometimes feel numb to God's presence? When you read the Scripture, does it seem dull and irrelevant? Are you restless during worship while those around you are enjoying the presence of God?

Then you, like all of us at one time or another, are in desperate need of a heart transplant. The only One able to perform this delicate operation is already here in the room, eager to hear your cry for help, ready to make you new and alive inside again.

Ask God to reveal any secret, hidden sins in your life that keep you from giving God rule and reign of your life.

EK LOVE Does someone you love need to repent and turn to God? True love calls for you to let that person know that you care. Tell him or her that God offers hope and renewal when we confess our sin.

> **Write a prayer …**
> for renewal and hope—for yourself, or members of your family, your church, or for your nation.

EK PRAYER Ezekiel deals with the collective sins of God's people and their failure to embody God's name, embrace His mission, and obey His Word. Pray that your church will know God's will and do it and make His name great.

EK KNOWLEDGE God's kingdom shines in moments like the ones Israel faced. Jerusalem had fallen. The temple had been burned and the city walls destroyed. Many of the survivors had been taken captive and carried off to Babylon.

Even in the worst circumstances, God offers His people hope and renewal. Sin has consequences, but God offers a new heart and a fresh start. Ezekiel 36 is full of promise.

> As you read this week's devotional thoughts and prepare for the next small-group session, for a more complete study, read Section 4, "His Kingdom Is," in *Empowering Kingdom Growth: The Heartbeat of God* (Nashville: Broadman & Holman, 2004).

God's Promises to His People

1. God promised permanence. God said that His people would "live in the land" (v. 28). They would not just return home for awhile. They would dwell there, abide there. God would cleanse Israel from their sin and give them His Spirit.

2. God promised growth and plenty. God said He would "summon the grain and make it plentiful" (v. 29). Desolate land would "become like the garden of Eden" (v. 35). Though our lives and our churches can languish for years in neglect and decay, God's Spirit can breathe new life into our hearts. This is your Father's desire for you.

3. God promised the spread of His kingdom. God's desire in redeeming us is to extend His kingdom's reach to others. In Ezekiel 36, God says, "the nations that remain around you will know that I, the LORD, have rebuilt what was destroyed and have replanted what was desolate. I, the LORD, have spoken and I will do it" (v. 36).

God wants to bring revival and fruitfulness to you and your church for one purpose—that those around you "will know that I am the LORD" (v. 38).

Discuss: Based on Ezekiel 36, what are some signs of revival in your heart?

What are some signs of revival in your church?

Scripture Text

Main Points

1.

2.

3.

Meaningful Illustrations

Personal Application

DAY 22 Finding Satisfaction

I was never a Rolling Stones fan, but I do remember their song "(I can't get no) Satisfaction." Its lyrics are nearly without rival in capturing the emptiness of humankind. This song—in its day—echoed the prevailing sentiments of a generation.

Has anything really changed over the years, though? We still see the many futile attempts people make—and we make—to find satisfaction. Bigger houses, better jobs, more money, faster cars, classier clothes, more outrageous and expensive thrills. These are all part of the quest to find satisfaction in life. We may call it fulfillment, happiness, or status, but we're all seeking to find meaning and purpose.

Satisfaction.

The miracle of the kingdom, though, is that when Jesus told us to pursue righteousness, to set our hearts on Him and His kingdom, He was actually offering us the only satisfaction life can give. In pursuing His kingdom, we discover that all the things we once considered worthy goals take a backseat to knowing God and experiencing the freedom that comes from His rule in our lives.

So do you want satisfaction? Then you want the kingdom because nothing else satisfies … though we try and we try and we try and we try.

This week read Jesus' Sermon on the Mount, chapters 5-7 in the Gospel of Matthew. How does Jesus' radical plan for finding satisfaction in life compare with what society says? How does it compare with your experiences ?

EK TRUTH

Spiritual Bankruptcy

I've walked with people through the experience of financial bankruptcy, so I understand the humiliation it causes. Spiritual bankruptcy ("poor in spirit") is a humbling experience, as well, but that's where the similarities end. There's no guarantee in bankruptcy that the person will ever recover financially. But Jesus promised that when we file for spiritual bankruptcy—when we recognize our complete inability to pay our debts or to dig ourselves out of the hole—the "kingdom of heaven" is ours (Matt. 5:3). We can bank on it.

To enjoy the satisfaction Jesus offers, we need to know what being "poor in spirit" is. It is the emptying of ourselves before God, humbly acknowledging our impoverished spiritual condition.

The more we recognize the enormous depth of our spiritual need, the more we will seek the reign of God in our lives. The less attached we are to this world, the more passionate we will become about the kingdom.

We struggle with this poor-in-spirit blessing because our world emphasizes self-reliance and self-confidence. We want to give the impression that we've got it all together. We've been led to believe that if we get enough education, lose enough weight, and develop a positive mental attitude, we will be happy. We have swallowed a lie that has left us empty.

Jesus' promise is unchanging truth; that's why the poor in spirit recognize the surpassing value of the kingdom. They are not ashamed to "become like children" in order to "enter the kingdom of heaven" (Matt. 18:3). They are the least and yet "the greatest in the kingdom" (Matt. 18:4). They have nothing but God, but they have all they want. They are satisfied. And we should long to be counted among their number.

How can you change to find real satisfaction?

**EK
KNOWLEDGE**

DAY 24

Satisfaction by Mourning

Here's another unexpected secret of satisfaction: " 'Blessed are those who mourn, because they will be comforted' " (Matt. 5:4).

Kingdom mourning is not depression but grief over our own spiritual bankruptcy. It is the result of seeing God in His holiness and seeing our own sinfulness in stark contrast. When confronted with God's purity, "those who mourn" are utterly stricken by the enormity of debt they owe.

This is the mourning of Isaiah, after seeing "the LORD seated on a high and lofty throne," angels encircling the room, the very foundation quaking beneath his feet, the whole temple filling with the smoke of God's glory. And without stopping for thought or explanation, Isaiah blurts out the only thing his soul knows to say: "Woe is me, for I am ruined, because I am a man of unclean lips and live among a people of unclean lips, and because my eyes have seen the King, the LORD of Hosts" (Isa. 6:1,5).

This was the experience of Paul, who cried out concerning his ongoing struggle with sin, "What a wretched man I am! Who will rescue me from this body of death?" (Rom. 7:24).

It is the experience of every kingdom citizen.

But—good news!—those who mourn over their sin are "comforted" by their forgiveness. While our awareness of need never departs, God's comfort is also continual. Our tears are tears of joy. We hurt, but we are satisfied.

This is more than a personal mourning. It's also a shared mourning— a sadness over the damaging effects of sin in our world, in our churches, in our extended families, among our friends. But for us, the sorrowing poor, our tears are turned into happy laughter through the intervention of the Messiah, whose kingdom pleasure is to "comfort all who mourn" (Isa. 61:2).

 Do you mourn today over the sins of your past? Over the sin of someone you love? Find comfort in knowing that through Jesus, God offers forgiveness. Continue to pray for those in sin.

EK LOVE

Meekness

Jesus said the meek, the gentle, would inherit the earth (Matt. 5:5). But our culture has created a different breed of inheritors. There is nothing remotely meek about the heroes of our day. Meekness and gentleness are not virtues we greatly admire, and this beatitude may not appeal to us.

In our minds meekness is often associated with weakness, passivity, or even cowardice. Or we may think it's simply a person's natural disposition, a tendency to be quiet and mellow, which some have and some don't. If either of these two is correct, (1) Jesus wouldn't have praised it, and (2) those of us who aren't so calm and collected by nature would be out of luck in satisfying Christ's command.

The Bible says that gentleness is a fruit of the Spirit (Gal. 5:23)—a Christlike character trait produced in the believer's life by the Holy Spirit. And furthermore, meekness is not weakness; it is power under control. Power restrained by gentleness. I like that.

We see this quality in Jesus. In the wilderness Satan offered Him all a man could want. Jesus could have had physical satisfaction, public acclaim, universal power. But He chose to submit to His Father. In Gethsemane, His human flesh begged to avoid the cross, but He submitted to the Father's eternal plan, " 'not what I will, but what You will' " (Mark 14:36). On the cross we see the supreme example of power under control. Do you remember the taunting cry of the criminal? "Aren't You the Messiah? Save Yourself and us!" (Luke 23:39). Everything in Jesus' human nature must have desired to come down and show them the fierce anger of the Lord. If we were there, we would have cheered if He had torn Himself free of the cross and taken His own revenge. But it was His meekness that held Him there, enabling Him to endure the shame and buy mankind's redemption.

EK COMMUNITY   Our ability to be meek—or not to be—is most often seen in our relationships with other people. When you're in difficult situations, are you in control of your emotions? Do you have meekness—power under control?

DAY 26 Hunger for God

The words hunger and thirst in Matthew 5:6 suggest a deep, profound, even painful desire that increases with desperation until it is fed.

That's how the kingdom citizen pursues righteousness—like a hungry man starving for supper, like a woman thirsty after an outdoor run—with an appetite that gets more ferocious all the time.

Our hunger for righteousness should be both recurring and ongoing. When we eat a sandwich at lunch, it may hold us for a while, but it doesn't satisfy our hunger for the rest of our lives. Our appetite for righteousness should keep growing. When we lose our appetite for the Lord and His kingdom, when we're just as content with the world's junk food as we are with the Word of God, something is wrong.

Kingdom hunger is
- an unquenchable desire to know Him;
- a desire to be free from sin because sin separates us from God;
- a desire to be free from the power of sin and controlled by God's Spirit;
- a desire to be free from the desire for sin and eager to please the Father;
- a desire to be like Jesus.

How do we seek righteousness? We let God show us who we really are. We do away with the pretense. As long as we think we're better than most, we are not hungry for righteousness. Spiritual fulfillment begins with an awareness of our spiritual bankruptcy. We must remove anything that dulls our spiritual appetite, whether it's overtly sinful or not. It might be NFL football, or boating, or a harmless hobby. But if it gets in the way of our pursuit of righteousness, it needs to go. Kingdom hunger demands it.

This requires real sacrifice, but it results in real satisfaction because those who orient their "hunger and thirst" in the direction of righteousness are guaranteed to find themselves "filled." When was the last time any sin left you feeling that way?

Are good things in your life keeping you away from the best God Has to offer? Seek His righteousness.

EK CHALLENGE

Salt and Light

Salty living means that we must embrace a lifestyle that is consistent with the character of our Father. It means that we will take seriously the demands of the beatitudes in our everyday life.

As kingdom people intent on obeying the Word of God, we know we cannot tread lightly upon these matters. As we hear Jesus begin to teach His disciples a few things about the way they should approach their religious activity, we too must listen reverently—and be prepared to obey completely—if we're to receive our Father's reward.

When salt loses its saltiness, it becomes useless to function as salt. Christianity can be just as useless without a lifestyle that embraces the teachings of the kingdom. Then our conduct doesn't become the fuel that makes our witness stand out like a light in the dark.

Jesus discussed three important aspects of kingdom living in the first part of Matthew 6—fasting, prayer, and giving.

- Fasting prepares us for powerful prayer.
- Prayer moves us to generosity.
- Generous giving provides visible evidence of our relationship to God.[1]

And for the benefit of all the rest of us who struggle with this from time to time—Jesus was not about to gloss over any one of these matters without confronting us on the issue of motive. The Pharisee prayed to be seen; the sinner prayed privately (Luke 18:9-14). Some gave for public acclaim; the widow quietly gave her all (Luke 21:1-4).

Salty behavior both demands and deserves illumination. Unless we explain the source of our righteousness, the world will never see the light.

Ask God to reveal to you your true motives for kingdom work. Are you salt and light?

EK PRAYER

---

[1] G. Campbell Morgan, *The Gospel According to Matthew* (New York: Fleming H. Revell Company, 1929), 59.

28 His Kingdom Is

Kingdom people hunger and thirst for kingdom activity in their lives.

When I was pastor at First Baptist Church in Norfolk, Virginia, we frequently called our congregation to prayer and fasting. One of our senior adults related how he had left the house at lunchtime on his way to church to pray. While he was praying, he became acutely aware of his physical hunger. He knew he had a fully stocked pantry waiting at home, once his fast was over. But in this kingdom moment, he realized he didn't have the same hunger for God that he did for food. His hunger for righteousness didn't gnaw at him with the same regularity and intensity as his hunger for breakfast, lunch, and dinner. Fasting and prayer are two aspects of New Testament kingdom life. Such hunger for righteousness is still needed today.

EK COMMUNITY

• Have you ever fasted or skipped a meal for a kingdom purpose?

• How is fasting for a kingdom purpose different from fasting for a diet or health reasons?

> U.S. Consumers spent more than $24.3 billion on candy in 2002, a 1.6% increase over 2001. In 2000 Americans spent $13 billion a year on chocolate. During 1999 U.S. soft drink sales came to $58 billion. In 2000 annual U.S. vending machine sales were $36 billion. U.S. gumball sales were at $500 million in 2000. In the first five months of 2004, 4,535,595 children under 5 had died in the world, mostly as a result of poverty.
> (Source: www.emptytomb.org)

• How did the experience sharpen your hunger for God and seeking His reign and rule in your life?

◆ Use the corresponding *EKG* DVD segment for this session at this point.

EK TRUTH

1. **Read Matthew 5:13.** It's confirmed: " 'You are the salt of the earth.' "

• What is the purpose of salt?

> **Salt Advisory**
> *"You are the salt of the earth. But if the salt should lose its taste, how can it be made salty? It's no longer good for anything but to be thrown out and trampled on by men"*
> (Matt. 5:13).

• List two ways kingdom people are like salt.

1.

2.

• Matthew 6:6 says, " 'Blessed are those who hunger and thirst for righteousness.' " Salt enhances the flavor of food and makes the hungry person want more. Eating salty food also makes people thirsty. How does your life make people hungry and thirsty for more of God?

• Recall someone in your life who has been for you " 'the salt of the earth,' " making you hunger and thirst for God. What was it about that person that made you want more of God?

✓

2. You are the light of the world. **Read "Lighten Up" (Matt. 5:14-15).**

- If kingdom citizens are the " 'light of the world,' " what is the source of that light?

> **Lighten Up**
> *"You are the light of the world. A city situated on a hill cannot be hidden. No one lights a lamp and puts it under a basket, but rather on a lampstand, and it gives light for all who are in the house"*
> (Matt. 5:14-15).

- John 8:12 says, " 'I am the light of the world. Anyone who follows Me will never walk in the darkness, but will have the light of life.' " What does it mean to you not to walk in darkness?

- How can you tell if your light is out there for all to see or if it is hidden?

- Think of examples of people who draw others to them. What characteristics do they have that attract people? Do these characteristics reflect "the Light of the world (Jesus)," or just a worldly light?

- Are you an active part of a community of believers? How does that affect your light and your lifestyle?

EK CHALLENGE Imagine the city on a hill. There are individual lights and the effect of all the lights together. When your light joins others, the combined light is brighter. How can you join your light with others to send it further into the dark?

EK LOVE

Being salt and light demands that we live in relationship with others. Is there a relationship you need to restore or one you need to begin in order to be salt and light for that person? This week plan a meal, have coffee, or make a phone call to begin that process.

EK PRAYER

Pray that you will be salt and light. Pray that you will make God's name great and bring others into the kingdom so that they too may know the benefits of kingdom living under the rule and reign of Christ.

EK KNOWLEDGE

SALT

Salt had many uses in Jesus' day. Therefore, when Jesus described His followers as being the " 'salt of the earth' " (Matt. 5:13), He must have triggered several different thoughts in the minds of His hearers.

> Less money is being saved or contributed to churches and charitable organizations, and more is being spent on credit card interest, recreation, alcohol, gambling (primarily through state lotteries) and pets. (Baptist Press) How does the way you spend your money reflect your ability to be salt and light?

1. Salt was a preservative. Without salt, how could the fish be preserved long enough to get it to the marketplace? In being described as "salt," Jesus' disciples knew He was challenging them to act like a preservative in a decaying world.

Discuss: How can Christians keep hope alive and culture from sinking?

2. Salt was an antiseptic. Salt disinfects. But, as you may know from experience, salt in a wound stings. We need to remember this. People may not understand or applaud our desire to help see them cleansed from the effects of sin through the salt of the gospel. They may demand tolerance or call us judgmental. But we must love people enough to help them heal, even if it hurts us and them.

Discuss: Is there a point at which a believer should stop trying to share the gospel or accept the rejection of someone who is lost?

3. Salt was also a catalyst for fire. In ancient Palestine people called their inverted earthen bowl ovens "earth(s)." Local salt was, and still is, mixed with dung and straw as fuel. People also lined the bottoms of their ovens with salt plates and threw handfuls of salt in the fire to raise the temperature. Over time, extreme heat causes salt to lose salinity and it becomes useless. This is why, in Luke 14:34-35, Jesus said that when salt had lost its saltiness, it was no longer fit for either the earth (the oven) or the dung hill (the fuel). The first followers of Jesus knew exactly what He was talking about. He was calling them to ignite spiritual fires on the earth, to be a helpful source of blessing in people's everyday lives.

> As you read this week's devotional thoughts and prepare for the next small-group session, for a more complete study, read Section 5, "His Kingdom Lives," in *Empowering Kingdom Growth: The Heartbeat of God* (Nashville: Broadman & Holman, 2004).

Discuss: In everyday tasks, with the lowliest of situations, how can you, as someone embodying Christ, make a difference?

LIGHT

Jesus used two different pictures to talk about the visibility of light.

1. A single light on a lampstand. Jesus said a lamp is not brought into a dark room to be hidden under a bed or a basket. It is to be put on a lampstand (Matt.5:15). Kingdom people may feel tempted by Satan to keep their witness quiet for whatever reason—guilt, bad timing, intellectual inferiority. But we should not be embarrassed. We do it for the King and for His kingdom. Your light will have the effect of a lamp upon a dark room.

2. The lights of the city on a hill. If you've ever been to a candlelight service, you've seen what happens when a single candle spreads its light to hundreds of others. Soon the entire room blazes with light. This image speaks to our need for Christian fellowship. When we join our light with the lights of other believers, we become that city set on a hill—more visible.

Discuss: How can you tell if your light is visible? What opportunities do you have to combine it with the testimonies and faith of others at church, work, school, or in your community?

---

[1]David S. Dockery and David E. Garland, *Seeking the Kingdom* (Wheaton: Harold Shaw Publishers, 1992), 36.

Scripture Text

Main Points

1.

2.

3.

Meaningful Illustrations

Personal Application

DAY 29 Jesus' Prayer

Read the prayer of Jesus carefully enough, and you begin to see that the kingdom of God breathes through every oft-quoted line and phrase.

Many commentators, in fact, agree that the Lord's Prayer is at the heart of the Sermon on the Mount and therefore at the heart of our Lord's teaching on the kingdom of God. If for no other reason than this, we should hunger afresh to understand its impact.

I can only say that studying the Lord's Prayer has changed my life. I came to it in the hopes that God would use it to improve my experience in prayer, and instead He has used it not only to alter my prayer life but to transform my view of the world. Through this powerful prayer, the Father has sensitized me to His kingdom activity and has given me the courage to participate with Him as He advances His kingdom through me.

I can't wait to see and hear what this prayer does in your life, as well.[1]

" 'Therefore, you should pray like this:

> Our Father in heaven,
> Your name be honored as holy.
> Your kingdom come.
> Your will be done
> on earth as it is in heaven.
> Give us today our daily bread.
> And forgive us our debts,
> as we also have forgiven our debtors.
> And do not bring us into temptation,
> but deliver us from the evil one.
> [For Yours is the kingdom and the power
> and the glory forever. Amen]' " (Matt. 16:9-13).

This week pray the Lord's Prayer, Jesus' prayer, with new awareness of the kingdom.

EK PRAYER

---

[1]I can only briefly summarize this prayer in the present work, but if your appetite has been whetted to know more, I recommend that you read my book, *The Prayer of Jesus* (Nashville: Broadman & Holman, 2001). Your church may also find the video study by the same name, produced by LifeWay Church Resources, to be a good follow-up to *Empowering Kingdom Growth*.

Our Father 30 DAY

We're probably so familiar with this opening line that the full impact of its radical nature doesn't startle us the way it did Jesus' first-century disciples. The intimacy of address Jesus used in approaching God as " 'Father' " is our first signal to the radical nature of this prayer. No one in Jesus' day would've ever dared address the Creator and King as " 'our Father.' " This level of personal intimacy with God was unheard of.

But it wasn't an accident on Jesus' part. Nor was it descriptive only of the relationship He had with the Father as the result of being His Son. For Jesus would later tell His disciples, " 'Anything you ask the Father in My name, He will give you' " (John 16:23).

All of His children were invited into this relationship.

This is the prayer of the child who knows that His Father's kingdom is paramount and thus His first desire is to advance the kingdom. It is the prayer of a child who knows His Father is trustworthy and therefore He submits to the will of the Father. It is the confident prayer that knows our Father is in the heavens.

Paul said that when we received the gift of the Holy Spirit, He gave us the right to cry out, "Abba, Father" (Rom. 8:15), a word that actually carries the meaning of our word *Daddy*. This is a testimony to God's love and grace, not an offensive devaluation of His holiness. It took a great God to stoop down to us, to desire to be our Father.

In the space provided, write a note thanking God for the privilege of calling Him Father.

EK LOVE

DAY 31
In Jesus' Name

What does it mean to pray in Jesus' name? It first means that we've established a personal relationship with God through His Son. But further, it means that we address the Father with the same commitment and mission as His Son. It means that His Son's passion has become our priority.

- It is the confident prayer of a child who knows his Father is in the heavens, far beyond all that we will ever comprehend, yet nonetheless so near that He knows what we need before we ask Him.
- This is the prayer of the child who knows his Father's name is holy and whose passion is to manifest the Father's holiness in his own life.
- It's the prayer of the child who knows that his Father's kingdom is paramount and whose first desire is to advance that kingdom.
- It's the prayer of the child who knows his Father is trustworthy, and therefore he submits his will to that of the Father.
- It's the prayer of the child whose only desire is to enjoy his Father's reward.

Two-thirds of the Lord's Prayer addresses the issues of the Father, and only one-third speaks of our personal needs. In thinking about my own prayer life, I realized that I had often reversed that order. I usually spent the largest amount of my prayer time on my own needs and wants.

But kingdom praying is not about informing God. He already knows!

Kingdom praying is not about convincing God to side with us. He already has! Kingdom praying is about enjoying God's presence and discovering His purpose.

Is this what you're already doing—or are you ready with all of your heart to start praying this way today?

 How does your awareness of the kingdom and of the intimate Father-child relationship you have with God make this prayer a personal experience rather than a ritual to repeat in corporate worship?

EK
KNOWLEDGE

Forgive Us

When Jesus taught His disciples to pray, He prayed: " 'Forgive us our debts, as we also have forgiven our debtors' " (Matt. 6:12). Do we honestly want God to forgive us in the same stingy way we often distribute our forgiveness to others? It truly is a chilling thought.

Forgiveness is at the heart of kingdom relationships. To begin with, we cannot become kingdom people at all without first experiencing the forgiveness of God.

Throughout our lives this recognition of God's holiness and our sinfulness continues to drive us to prayer, seeking our Father's forgiveness. As kingdom children, we place so much value on the intimacy we enjoy with our Dad, we can't allow anything to hinder our relationship—even for a brief moment. We need forgiveness and we know it. So we go to our Father in prayer.

Have you ever thought that prayer is really a family affair—not just conversation between Father and child but also a way to remind ourselves that we are members of the family of God, that we are in community with one another? In all of the statements of request found in the Lord's Prayer, all of the pronouns Jesus used are plural: " 'Give us today our daily bread.' " " 'Do not bring us into temptation.' " " 'Deliver us from the evil one.' "

We don't just pray for ourselves. We pray for one another.

And the request for forgiveness is no different. " 'Forgive us our debts, as we also have forgiven our debtors.' "

So for the same reason that I cannot pray for my own "daily bread" while remaining unconcerned for my brother's lack of bread, I cannot receive God's forgiveness for myself without being prepared to dispense an equal portion to others. Forgiveness must go both ways in our lives, or we're not going anywhere in the kingdom.

EK COMMUNITY

Pray for others' needs as well as your own. Ask God to reveal those needs to you so that you can pray specifically.

DAY 33 Forever

Look around you. What in your world is eternal? Your diploma? Your home entertainment system? Your week at the beach every summer?

The only thing that's truly eternal around you and me today is people—human beings whose souls will live on after they die.

Some will be redeemed and will live forever. Some will be lost and will face God's righteous judgment. But putting our energies into serving, helping, loving, encouraging, and supporting other people is how kingdom people invest in eternity.

Our money is God's money, and it's intended to be used to advance His eternal kingdom. But storing " 'treasure in heaven' " is so much more than just putting money in an offering plate. It's about investing in our children rather than loading them up with gifts and gadgets. It's about investing in our families rather than filling all our free time with pleasure. It's about investing in our neighbors rather than sinking all our time and money into the lawn and the landscaping.

It's not wrong to possess earthly things, but we can't let earthly things possess us. Money itself doesn't pose a threat to the kingdom person. But those who love it will always struggle when called upon to share it.

How do we claim victory in this area of our lives? We begin by acknowledging that we possess nothing. We determine that our role in regard to money is to manage it for God, the real owner.

We look for opportunities to invest in forever through our church, our denomination, and other missions organizations that are advancing God's kingdom. We become involved personally and financially with relief organizations in our own communities.

We let the Eternal control our checkbook.

EK CHALLENGE

Learning about the kingdom is exciting, but joining God at work in the world is even more exciting. How will you redirect your finances to join God's kingdom activity?

No More Worry

34

DAY

Do you think it's possible to live without anxiety? Would you like to do so? Five times in the 10 verses, Matthew 6:25-34, Jesus used the word worry. And in three of these instances, He spoke it as a command: " 'Don't worry.' " He wasn't merely making a suggestion or trying to calm people down. This was an order! "Worry," He said, should be banned from the hearts of kingdom people.

Why is it wrong for kingdom people to be fraught with worry?
1. Worry is futile and counterproductive. Jesus pointedly asked whether anxiety could add even a short time to our life spans (v. 27). In truth, doctors tell us that anxiety will most likely shorten our lives.
2. Worry indicates a lack of understanding. The nature and character of our Father is to feed the songbirds and water the wildflowers. " 'Aren't you worth more than they?' " (v. 26). To fail to trust God is to doubt Him.
3. Worry shows a lack of faith. Jesus said it takes a person " 'of little faith' " to worry about His needs being met (v. 30). What impact does anxiety have on our kingdom witness?
4. Worry is an ungodly response to life. Of all the arguments against anxiety, this one should perhaps stun us. If worry is the pattern that comes most naturally to everyone (v. 32), why would we want to be known for being like the average unbeliever?

As kingdom people, there should be numerous things about us that can only be explained by the presence of the Holy Spirit. Freedom from worry is one of them.

EK TRUTH

When I pray "Thy kingdom come," I am establishing that my first concern each day is God's kingdom and not mine. Further, I am asking the Father to show me what He is doing and allow me to participate with Him as He advances His kingdom on earth. Ask God to strengthen your faith and put your focus on the kingdom so that you can put worry behind you.

35 His Kingdom Lives

You can have an intimate relationship with the King of the universe.

My youngest daughter went off to college a few years ago. Her first semester phone bill was higher than her tuition. She called me every day. I'd be driving down the road, the phone would ring, and I would think: *Something's wrong. She's sick. She needs money.*

"How are you doing, honey?"

"Fine."

"Need money?"

"No."

"Why did you call, babe?"

"Daddy, I just wanted to say I love you."

You know what I did? I bought her a cell phone—unlimited minutes, no roaming charges.

I want you to understand something. The Sovereign Creator of the universe has given you a cell phone—unlimited minutes, any time, anywhere, no roaming charges. He said, "listen, I'm always here for you."

Imagine. The Sovereign King of the universe chooses to communicate with the people in His kingdom.

> My desire to know more about the kingdom of God began in earnest because Jesus drew attention to the kingdom—His hunger for the kingdom, His daily awareness of the kingdom, His confidence in the kingdom.
>
> How has your awareness of God's kingdom already changed your prayer life?

EK COMMUNITY

- Why is it you experience greater security and less worry by knowing that with a cell phone you can reach those you love and they can reach you quickly?

- Do you feel the same or greater sense of security knowing that you can always talk to God?

◆ Use the corresponding *EKG* DVD segment for this session at this point

EK TRUTH

1. Read Matthew 6:9-13.
- Name some ways you can honor your heavenly Father.

- Calling God "Father" is an intimate thing to do. It's one thing to know God as Creator and King, and another to be His people and part of His kingdom. But what are some of your feelings about being told that He is also our heavenly Father, and that He knows about and is involved in our personal needs and relationships? List and discuss.

> **How to Talk to Your Father**
> "Therefore, you should pray like this:
>
> Our Father in heaven,
> Your name be honored as holy.
> Your kingdom come.
> Your will be done
> on earth as it is in heaven.
> Give us today our daily bread.
> And forgive us our debts,
> as we also have forgiven our debtors.
> And do not bring us into temptation,
> but deliver us from the evil one.
> [For Yours is the kingdom and the power
> and the glory forever. Amen]
> (Matt. 6:9-13).

- Find actions in this prayer to embody God's name, embrace God's mission, and obey God's Word.

Embody _____

Embrace _____

Obey _____

- Praying for daily needs requires daily prayer. How does it make you feel to know that God expects you, at any and all times, to come to Him for personal conversation?

- Kingdom praying is personal communication with God based on Who He is, as the Almighty Ruler of everything, and who you are, as His child, creation, and possession. What is the purpose of "kingdom" praying?

- If you wanted someone to pray for you, whom would you call? Why?

EK CHALLENGE

Make Jesus' prayer personal in your own life. Ask yourself the following.

- Are you satisfied with just enough daily bread for today?

- Do you honor your Father's name, represent Him well wherever you go?

- Do you really want God to forgive you in proportion to your willingness to forgive others?

Troubled Times

During 2003, while 84% of adults say their religious faith is very important in their own life, 66% also say that religion is losing influence in the nation. While people are spending less time in religious practices such as Bible reading, prayer, and church activities, 70% claim that their own faith is growing deeper. At the same time that 84% of adults claim to be Christian, 75% say they are either absolutely or somewhat committed to Christianity, and 60% say they believe the Bible is totally accurate, the moral foundations of the nation are crumbling with increases in those who contend that cohabitation (60%), adultery (42%), sexual relations between homosexuals (30%), abortion (45%), pornography (38%), profanity (36%) and gambling (61%) are "morally acceptable." (Source: Barna Research Online)

EK LOVE

Talk regularly with your heavenly Father, just to tell Him you love Him. Make that a habit in your prayer life this week.

EK PRAYER

Call three people and ask how you can pray for them this week.

Pray the Lord's Prayer daily with new meaning and a kingdom awareness.

EK KNOWLEDGE

HIS HOLY NAME

Jesus taught the eternal truth; His Father's name is holy. We know this from the Lord's Prayer, for example. Discuss the following facts about the holiness of Gods name.

- When we pray "hallowed be thy name," or quote, "Your name be honored as holy," we are not giving God permission for His name to be holy. His name is holy already. We're asking for His name to be made holy in our lives.

- When Jews came to the name *YHWH* (Jehovah) in the Scripture text, they would not speak it aloud.

- In the Book of Revelation, we are told that the living creatures around the Father's throne never cease in crying, "Holy, holy, holy, Lord God, the Almighty, who was, who is, and who is coming" (4:8). So we're not asking for God's name to be made holy in its very nature. It already is!

> **Testimony**
> I received Christ as my personal Savior when I was nine years of age. In that moment, as I prayed to accept Christ into my heart, my sins were forgiven, I was transferred from the kingdom of darkness into the kingdom of life, and my home in heaven was assured.
>
> But I can see in my mind's eye one other significant event that occurred. Jesus took me by the hand and led me into the presence of sovereign God. He whispered to me, "Look, Ken, some call him Yahweh, the God of covenant faithfulness. But I just call him Dad. And now that you're in relationship with me, you too can climb up into his lap and address him as Dad."

"When they came to the nations where they went, they profaned [His] holy name" (Ezek. 36:20). The nations concluded—by looking at His people's conduct and behavior—that God's name was not holy, or hallowed.

As you read this week's devotional thoughts and prepare for the next small-group session, for a more complete study, read Section 6, "His Kingdom Never Ends," in *Empowering Kingdom Growth: The Heartbeat of God* (Nashville: Broadman & Holman, 2004).

• In Jesus' farewell prayer before going to the cross, He told the Father, "I have revealed Your name to the men You gave Me from the world" (John 17:6). Every action, word, and deed of His life was built around a singular focus—to reveal His Father's name and His holiness. In other words, Jesus succeeded where God's people, both then and now, frequently fail.

THY KINGDOM COME

Our kingdom purpose couldn't be clearer than when we pray in the Lord's Prayer, "Thy kingdom come." The final consummation of the kingdom is an established, biblical fact. So our prayer that God's kingdom will "come" is an appeal for its reality to be evident in our daily lives.

Are you aware of being a kingdom citizen every day? How and why?

When I pray "Thy kingdom come," I am establishing that my first concern each day is God's kingdom and not mine. Further, I am asking the Father to show me what He is doing and allow me to participate with Him as He advances His kingdom on earth.

• Give an example of when God did or could use you for His purpose.

Once when I was reading this verse—John 5:20—I was prompted to ask the Father why He didn't show me everything He was doing around me. His response was profound but convicting: I had never really asked Him to.

Have you?

Scripture Text

Main Points

1.

2.

3.

Meaningful Illustrations

Personal Application

DAY 36 Kingdom Keys

Keys, like gates, are a biblical symbol of authority (Isa. 22:22). And Jesus has given the "keys of the kingdom"—the power and authority of God—to His community, the church. " 'I will give you the keys of the kingdom of heaven, and whatever you bind on earth is already bound in heaven, and whatever you loose on earth is already loosed in heaven' " (Matt. 16:19).

This doesn't make us the doorkeeper that decides who gets in but more of a steward who has the authority to show that these keys are real, that they work, that they do indeed lead to life.

The best way I know to describe the "keys" is to think of them as the message of the gospel, which is the only way to be given acceptance into the kingdom. Jesus entrusted these keys into the hands of His apostles, who used them to open the door of faith for both Jew and Gentile alike.

And today these keys are in our hands, placed there by virtue of our relationship with Jesus Christ.

God has chosen the church to declare His message and uphold His truth. The church is God's kingdom people in community. This is why every kingdom person must of necessity identify himself with the church, using his gifts and resources to advance its work as it in turn advances the kingdom.

The King has called.
The dying await.
The gates tremble.
The kingdom comes.

Take out the keys from your pocket or purse. Look at them. What doors do they open for you? What in your life gives you access to kingdom work?

EK CHALLENGE

Holy Spirit Power 37 DAY

Everything is about the kingdom, just as Paul demonstrated by continually "engaging in discussion and trying to persuade [others] about the things related to the kingdom of God" (Acts 19:8).

Even in our last glimpse of him at the unfinished ending of the Book of Acts, he was awaiting trial in Rome, living in a rented house, "proclaiming the kingdom of God and teaching the things concerning the Lord Jesus Christ with full boldness and without hindrance" (Acts 28:31).

This is the heartbeat of the church—now as well as then.

We have not outgrown this heyday of kingdom advance. We continue to live in days that are ripe for reaching our neighborhoods and nation with the gospel of Jesus Christ, experiencing His kingdom fruit in our daily lives, sending and supporting missionaries around the globe, and praying for those who are embodying Christ to the unsaved people of the world.

We are fully able to embrace God's kingdom priorities as His community on earth: proclaiming Christ's redemption, establishing new churches, united and made up of diverse types of people, teaching sound doctrine, enjoying true fellowship, giving ourselves to worship, and expecting God to work among us. But it takes more than wanting to. It takes more than wishing it could be so. It even takes more than our best efforts, our keenest planning, and our bulldog determination.

It takes Holy Spirit power.

EK COMMUNITY Who in your neighborhood needs a word from God today? Ask God to show you where He is at work in your world. Seek the Holy Spirit's power. Join God in His work.

DAY 38 All We Need

How do we mere mortals dare think that we can advance the kingdom of God on earth? Since few of us ever hope to attain greatness in the eyes of the world, we just don't consider ourselves all that powerful or influential. It's overwhelming for most of us to think we could actually be involved in daily conversations and actions that will impact eternity.

But every Christian who lives with kingdom purpose can know true greatness. And this is why: "for thine is the power!" (see Matt. 6:13). God is all powerful. We can't, but He will!

Truly, living with kingdom purpose by relying on God's power is the only way we will ever see lasting, spiritual fruit growing from the things we do or say. Any other approach is destined for a temporary shelf life and guaranteed insignificance.

We must let God inspire and direct us if we are to perform His kingdom purposes. Genuine kingdom growth and ministry requires supernatural empowering.

Kingdom people are not given an option about being entrusted with God's power and His message. The Holy Spirit is given to us, lives within us, and produces all the necessary power to propel our witness.

The Holy Spirit is God in us, enabling us to advance God's kingdom, to serve His purpose and do His will.

With God living in and through us, we have everything we need.

EK PRAYER

How has discussing and learning about God's kingdom changed you? Write a prayer in the space provided as you talk with God about your role in His kingdom.

Kingdom Fruit

39 DAY

The Holy Spirit not only provides the power for witness. He also produces the fruit of holiness. We don't make ourselves pure and righteous before God in any other way. The Holy Spirit alone enables us to obey.

In submitting our will to His way—in surrendering the short-term glory of our kingdom for the eternal reward of the Father—the Spirit spontaneously produces in us "love, joy, peace, patience, kindness, goodness, faith, gentleness, self-control" (Gal. 5:22-23).

These are character traits we can't work up on our own. Oh, we may be able to dabble around the edges and display them at one time or another. But only the Spirit can make these an ongoing experience in our lives.

Remember, God is searching for a people who will display His character. And He has given us His Holy Spirit to produce His character through us.

 Consider ways you would like to demonstrate the fruit of the Spirit in your own life as you ask God to work through you.

EK LOVE

love_____

joy _____

peace _____

patience _____

kindness _____

goodness _____

faith _____

gentleness_____

self-control_____

40 The Rest of the Story

His story is far from over.

We live now in the overlap of the ages that theologians call the "already and not yet." We are already experiencing kingdom fullness as believers in Christ, but we are still looking forward to a future brand of kingdom fullness. We have a taste, but it has only whetted our appetite for more, compelling us to extend His kingdom by sharing the gospel, planting new believers in thriving churches, and teaching modern-day disciples to obey the King. Every day we live with this forever reality burning inside us.

We set off into each morning with Jesus, the Hope of our world, communicating His truth to us through His Word and by His Spirit. We enter every personal encounter by recognizing the possibility that we are staring a kingdom opportunity in the face. We are filled with a joy that has transformed flesh and bone into salt and light.

Kingdom living comes in the death of our pride, our sin, our greed, our fears, our selfish wants. It will cost us our desire to be left alone, our tight rein over our schedule of entertainment, our discomfort with anything more than hit-and-miss, here-and-there, cut-and-dried Christianity.

It will change us. We will read the Bible with a new appetite for holiness, with the fresh air of genuine gratitude, with the deep-seated assurance that our souls have been bought and paid for at the cost of Christ's blood.

We will want to be like Him. We will want to be with Him. We will want to be among His people in kingdom community, and we will want to tell the good news to everyone we meet. We are living in kingdom days, alive as God's kingdom people.

Nothing is more important. Nothing holds more promise. And nothing can stop us now. We are children of the King!

EK TRUTH

Review Scriptures you have seen in a new way in this study. How has this experience changed the way you view God's word? How has it changed the way you see the world? How has it changed your desire to be an active kingdom person at work in the world?

His Kingdom Never Ends

All things will come to an end—except the kingdom of God.

It was 1991. We were at war. A large number of members from our church in Norfolk had been dispatched to the Persian Gulf for Operation Desert Storm. These were turbulent days for those in our naval community, and we wanted to minister to them. I knew the sermon I was preparing for the following Sunday morning was critical. Many would come to hear what God's people had to say about the outbreak of hostilities, wanting a word from the Lord to put them at peace and give them hope and trust.

I was scheduled to preach from Matthew 16:18: " 'On this rock I will build My church, and the forces of Hades will not overpower it.' " And I was having some reservations about the appropriateness of this text, which I had chosen months earlier. I'll never forget what my friend Dick Baker said. "I've heard you preach on this text before. When you talk about this, don't you say that the decisions made in the life of the church have greater eternal significance than any decision made in the halls of Washington, D.C.?" I admitted that this would definitely be part of the message. "If you believe that," he said, "then why would you think of changing it? That is precisely what we need to hear!"

EK COMMUNITY What in your life has ended that you thought would never end? (a relationship, a job, good health, a move from a home, a closed business or church)

 Use the corresponding *EKG* DVD segment for this session at this point

1. Read Matthew 16:13-19, then answer and discuss.

EK TRUTH

• Who did people say that Jesus was?

• Who do people today say that Jesus is?

• Do you have a "rock"? What is it?

• If you were asked to confess your faith as Peter did, what would you say?

• How does your confession affect the way you live?

> **Recognition**
> *When Jesus came to the region of Caesarea Philippi, He asked His disciples, " 'Who do people say that the Son of Man is?' "*
>
> *And they said, "Some say John the Baptist; others, Elijah; still others, Jeremiah or one of the prophets."*
>
> *" 'But you,' " He asked them, " 'who do you say that I am?' "*
>
> *Simon Peter answered, "You are the Messiah, the Son of the living God!"*
>
> *And Jesus responded, " 'Simon son of Jonah, you are blessed because flesh and blood did not reveal this to you, but My Father in heaven. And I also say to you that you are Peter, and on this rock I will build My church, and the forces of Hades will not overpower it. I will give you the keys of the kingdom of heaven, and whatever you bind on earth is already bound in heaven, and whatever you loose on earth is already loosed in heaven' "* (Matt. 16:13-19).

• How do you think the kingdom and the church relate?

2. Read Acts 28:23-31. This is an interesting glimpse into the final years of Paul's life and ministry.

- At the end of his ministry, in house arrest, how did Paul spend his time?

- What did he preach?

- What response did he get?

- Do you know anyone whose heart seems to be hardened?

- Who in today's world would you compare to the Jews, the people God chose for His own? Who would you compare to the Gentiles, the non-Jews?

- Where do you see God at work in the world today?

The Witness

After arranging a day with him, many came to him at his lodging. From dawn to dusk he expounded and witnessed about the kingdom of God. He persuaded them concerning Jesus from both the Law of Moses and the Prophets. Some were persuaded by what he said, but others did not believe.

Disagreeing among themselves, they began to leave after Paul made one statement: "The Holy Spirit correctly spoke through the prophet Isaiah to your forefathers when He said,
Go to this people and say:
'You will listen and listen,
yet never understand;
and you will look and look,
yet never perceive.
For this people's heart
has grown callous,
their ears are hard of hearing,
and they have shut their eyes;
otherwise
they might see with their eyes
and hear with their ears,
understand with their heart,
and be converted—
and I would heal them.'
Therefore, let it be known to you that this saving work of God has been sent to the Gentiles; they will listen!" [After he said these things, the Jews departed, while engaging in a prolonged debate among themselves.].
Acts 28:23-29

EK CHALLENGE

How will you allow the kingdom of God to make a difference in your life? in your home? in your church?

EK LOVE

How will you embody God's name, embrace His mission, and obey His Word?

EK PRAYER

Are members of your family members of the kingdom? Each generation could be the last to know the good news of Jesus Christ unless this generation, like Paul, tells people about Jesus. What are you doing to ensure that the next generation knows about Jesus, the things He taught about the kingdom of God?

Invested?

In 2001 Easter holiday sales were expected to be $2.8 billion.

In 1999 overseas ministries income to more than 600 agencies, including denomination, interdenominational, and independent agencies was $2.9 billion. (Source: emptytomb.org)

What do statistics reveal about where people invest their money?

Describe a good "kingdom" investment.

What kingdom investments have you made?

Pray that God will show you where He is at work in the world and that He will reveal kingdom opportunities to you.

EK KNOWLEDGE

MATTHEW 16

Two things make this passage powerful. One is the confession of Peter, "You are the Messiah, the Son of the living God!" (v. 16). Matthew alone recorded the second half of Peter's statement. This phrase—"the Son of the living God"—declared that Jesus had a special relationship with the Father, that He was more than the Savior of one group but the Savior of all. We can almost imagine Jesus saying, "My role was to show you the Father through My life and words, and I have succeeded. You have recognized the family resemblance."

Think about how much you resemble God's family. Who do you know that can you really see Jesus in?

Responding to the lightning strike of Peter's bold assertion, Jesus added the second punch: "On this rock I will build My church, and the forces of Hades will not overpower it" (v. 18).

Throughout the Old Testament, *rock* was a visual symbol of God (Deut. 32:4; Ps. 18:2,31). And here we see the Rock in human form—Jesus of Nazareth, "the Son of the living God"—preparing to "build" something more powerful, alive, and indestructible than anything the world had ever seen. Jesus Himself was going to construct it on His own strong shoulders, equip it with authority, and launch it into human history with both might and a mission.

JESUS PICKS A NAME FOR US

With a new twist on an old name Jesus named us *ekklesia*. The Greeks used this term to refer to the assembly of its free men in the cities. The Old Testament Scriptures had used a similar term to refer to the "congregation" or "community," which marked Israel as a select, God-governed people.

Now Jesus was transforming this word into a new idea—the church!

Not equating the church with the kingdom of God, Jesus initiated it as His primary instrument for advancing the kingdom. He would entrust it with the timeless message of His redemption and enable it to carry the torch of truth.

And His church would change the world.

Your Kingdom Covenant
Have you ever wanted just the right words to express something? Hopefully, after participating in A 40 Day Experience: EKG, The Heartbeat of God, you sense God leading you, calling you, to acknowledge His love for you and yours for Him. Inside the back cover you will find a personal covenant card that will help you express your personal response to your Father, Who rules and reigns.

Sermon Notes / **His Kingdom Never Ends**

Scripture Text

Main Points

1.

2.

3.

Meaningful Illustrations

Personal Application

How to Become a Christian

Some people think a personal relationship with God is something they could never have. Actually, God's desire to save you and show you how much He loves you makes this relationship available to you. Here it is, explained in three steps.

Admit

Admit to God that you are a sinner. This is the first step in turning from sin and turning toward God. Each of us has a problem the Bible calls sin. Sin is a refusal to acknowledge God's authority over our lives. Everyone who does not live a life of perfect obedience to the Lord is guilty of sin. "For all have sinned and fall short of the glory of God" (Rom. 3:23). Since none of us is perfect, all of us are sinners (Rom. 3:10-18). Because, by God's perfect standard, everyone is guilty, we are all subject to eternal punishment for sin (Rom. 6:23). Everyone needs be saved, or rescued, because sin condemns everyone. Admit that you are a sinner and need God's help.

Believe

Believe in Jesus Christ as God's Son and receive Jesus' gift of forgiveness from sin. God loves each of us. God offers us salvation. Although we have done nothing to deserve His love and salvation. God wants to save us. In the death of Jesus on the cross, God provided salvation for all who would repent, or turn, from their sins and believe and follow Jesus. " 'For God loved the world in this way: He gave His One and Only Son, so that everyone who believes in Him will not perish but have eternal life' " (John 3:16).

Confess

Confess your faith in Jesus Christ as Savior and Lord. This means when you have received Jesus Christ into your life, tell others about it. Tell your pastor or a Christian friend about your decision. Follow Christ's example and ask for baptism by immersion in your local church as a public statement of your faith. "If you confess with your mouth, 'Jesus is Lord,' and believe in your heart that God raised Him from the dead, you will be saved. With the heart one believes, resulting in righteousness, and with the mouth one confesses, resulting in salvation" (Rom. 10:9-10).

Ideas for Leading
Small-Group Sessions

SESSION CHARACTERISTICS

Small-group sessions in this 40 Day Experience are designed with these characteristics:

Open to anyone who wants to participate. Questions and content assume that both Christians and seekers, church members and potential members, will participate together in these sessions.

Insight driven. Many Bible study groups are content driven: participants learn from reading and hearing a teacher-leader. In A 40 Day Experience resource, by contrast, the sessions are insight driven. That means insights about the Scriptures, applications, and questions are valued from all participants and should be encouraged. Everyone has the same handbook with icons that point out whether the interactive parts can be expected to help members know each other, apply biblical truths to life, understand Scriptures and their background, or invite them to pray. Participants in the group learn from one another in the small groups sessions, often bringing additional insights from the daily devotionals.

Designed so the leader can be a member of the group, and any group member can be the leader. Because the small-group process in this resource does not depend on someone to prepare and share information, less advance preparation is needed. The leader is a guide and facilitator.

The Leader's Role

1. *To get to know members of the small group*—Trust and closeness tend to build in the small group throughout the 40 days. The leader's knowing and being sensitive to group members will ensure that everyone in the session can be comfortable. If your group members don't know each other well and a particular question might cause awkwardness, encourage members to write their responses. Then call for volunteers to respond aloud.

2. *To encourage everyone to participate*—The quietest member may have the deepest insights but share them only with encouragement, or when everyone else has spoken. On the other hand, if some members tend to dominate the sessions, the leader may need to interrupt politely and say,

"Thanks for adding to the discussion. I want to be sure we get to hear from some of the others who might be ready to contribute."

3. **To be comfortable with silence**—Allow participants time to think. Encourage others to speak. The leader's responsibility is not to step in and share insights or content as much as it is to create a comfortable environment for all to participate.

4. **To affirm all learners**—Because the content is insight driven, all members should be affirmed when they respond. When members do not see a passage of Scripture the same way or have not had the same experience, they can learn from one another.

5. **To prepare by reading the session and devotionals, and watching the DVD**—The leader should go over the materials before the session. Be sensitive to what God might do in the group. Don't lecture. Pray for the Holy Spirit's leadership in the group.

6. **To plan the flow of the session so that all parts are covered**—Each session has multiple parts, beginning with material that introduces the topic and helps participants begin to interact. A corresponding *EKG* DVD segment (found in the *EKG, The Heartbeat of God Leader Kit*), featuring Ken Hemphill, provides 8-10 minutes of focused teaching on the topic to help facilitators lead and enrich group discussion. Have a time frame for moving the group through the session.

Beginning

A brief introduction frames the topic of each session. Invite someone in the group to read it aloud, or invite participants to read silently down to the first activity icon and then do the activity. Continue this pattern through the rest of the session.

The Icons

The diamond indicates the suggested time to use an 8-10 minute DVD segment from the *EKG Leader Kit*. The author introduces each session topic to the group. The purpose of the DVD segments are to help facilitators lead the group and to direct and enrich group discussions in the sessions.

EK COMMUNITY *EK Community* uses questions to help group members learn about one another. These are intended to break the ice, engage people, and encourage them to interact.

EK TRUTH

EK Truth denotes activities that guide group members to examine Bible passages. Participants should be encouraged to apply Scriptures to their lives and share their insights on Scripture. Although people with knowledge of the Bible are helpful resources, each person's thoughts are important.

EK CHALLENGE

EK Challenge icons are there to challenge group members to apply specific Bible verses to their lives and take action. Hopefully, insights brought up in the group will lead to boldness and risk in group members living out God's commands and instructions.

EK LOVE

EK Love symbols appear with suggestions of ways for group members to show Christ-like love and concern for one another and for people outside their small group.

EK PRAYER

EK Prayer is the sign that directs participants to pray about needs revealed during a session or devotional. Group members will be encouraged to talk with God about things that come up in the study and in their lives.

**EK
KNOWLEDGE**

EK Knowledge signals ways to help group members think about and understand the meaning of Scriptures during the session and in the devotionals.

The Sermon Notes Pages

Each small-group session is followed by a sermon notes page. Because pastors are encouraged to preach on the session topics, these pages become tools to help capture the content and insights from God through the pastor's message.

CHRISTIAN GROWTH STUDY PLAN

In the **Christian Growth Study Plan (formerly Church Study Course),** this book A 40 Day Experience: *EKG, The Heartbeat of God:* is a resource for course credit in the subject area Personal Life of the Christian Growth category of plans. To receive credit, read the book, complete the learning activities, show your work to your pastor, a staff member or church leader, then complete the following information. This page may be duplicated. Send the completed page to:

Christian Growth Study Plan
One LifeWay Plaza • Nashville, TN 37234-0117
• **FAX: (615) 251-5067**
• **E-mail:** *cgspnet@lifeway.com*
For information about the Christian Growth Study Plan, refer to the Christian Growth Study Plan Catalog. It is located online at *www.lifeway.com/cgsp.* If you do not have access to the Internet, contact the Christian Growth Study Plan office (1.800.968.5519) for the specific plan you need for your ministry.

EKG, THE HEARTBEAT OF GOD
COURSE NUMBER: CG-1062

PARTICIPANT INFORMATION

Social Security Number (USA ONLY-optional)　Personal CGSP Number*　Date of Birth (MONTH, DAY, YEAR)

Name (First, Middle, Last)　Home Phone

Address (Street, Route, or P.O. Box)　City, State, or Province　Zip/Postal Code

Please check appropriate box:　❑ Resource purchased by self　❑ Resource purchased by church　❑ Other

CHURCH INFORMATION

Church Name

Address (Street, Route, or P.O. Box)　City, State, or Province　Zip/Postal Code

CHANGE REQUEST ONLY

❑ Former Name

❑ Former Address　City, State, or Province　Zip/Postal Code

❑ Former Church　City, State, or Province　Zip/Postal Code

Signature of Pastor, Conference Leader, or Other Church Leader　Date

*New participants are requested but not required to give SS# and date of birth. Existing participants, please give CGSP# when using SS# for the first time. Thereafter, only one ID# is required. **Mail to:** Christian Growth Study Plan, One LifeWay Plaza, Nashville, TN 37234-0117. Fax: (615)251-5067.

Rev. 3-03

Also Available!

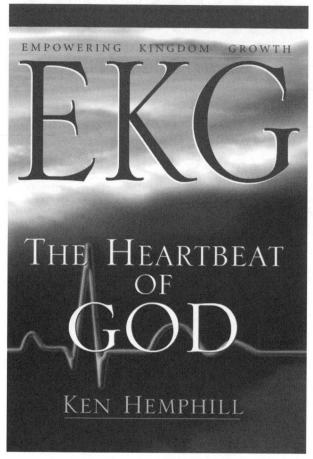

0-8054-3147-0, $19.99

Empowering Kingdom Growth
The Heartbeat of God
by Ken Hemphill

This life-changing book about the meaning and power of God's kingdom is the basis for *A 40 Day Experience: EKG*. Ken Hemphill, who's impact has been felt as an author, pastor and seminary president, explains how God's deep passion for us gives us the key to a life with eternal purpose and meaning in the hardback book *Empowering Kingdom Growth*.